SPECIAL THANKS TO:

PATRICIA EAGLE - my editor - for making sense of my words, correcting my grammar and for being delicate with your criticism. I probably screwed this part up because I added it after you were finished!

LORINN RHODES - our photographer - for snapping so many great pictures of my family.

SUSAN MEESKE - the real talent at the Leadership Difference - for everything.

AND MOST OF ALL...

LORI, BROOKE AND SLADE MITCHELL for supporting the travels and musings of a man pursuing happiness. I love you all so much.

LAUGH AND LEARN!

LIVE AND LEARN
OR DIE STUPID

LIVE AND LEARN OR DIE STUPID!

The Struggle for Happiness

DAVE MITCHELL

Bloomington, IN Milton Keynes, UK

authorHOUSE

AuthorHouse™
1663 Liberty Drive, Suite 200
Bloomington, IN 47403
www.authorhouse.com
Phone: 1-800-839-8640

AuthorHouse™ UK Ltd.
500 Avebury Boulevard
Central Milton Keynes, MK9 2BE
www.authorhouse.co.uk
Phone: 08001974150

First published by AuthorHouse 7/6/2006

ISBN: 1-4259-4398-5 (sc)
ISBN: 1-4259-4397-7 (dj)

Library of Congress Control Number: 2006905300

Printed in the United States of America
Bloomington, Indiana

This book is printed on acid-free paper.

CONTENTS

PREFACE

(Who the heck is Dave Mitchell?)

I'm just an average guy. Occasionally I feel different, unique, or special in some fundamental way, but when you get right down to it, I recognize we are all pretty similar. Most of us don't walk on hot coals every morning to get motivated about our jobs, although many of us feel about that much pain when we arrive at work. Try as we might, repeating affirmations into the mirror won't change the fact that several of us are quite unsettled by the sight of our own face and body.

No supreme being shows me signs when I am troubled. I am an average person. So are you, I'm guessing. We fall in that broad range called normal. Bottom line, the pursuit of happiness for many of us is the most difficult undertaking we will ever face. In fact, sometimes I think it is impossible for most of us to just be content.

I am not a behavioral psychologist. I am not a self-help guru. I have no magical formula, product, tape series, theory, breakthrough, diet, substance, pill, stretching exercise, or workout regimen. I have not talked to God. Not any of them. I am in no way more qualified to examine the concept of happiness than the clerk at my favorite wine store, or my high school baseball coach, or my father, or the customer service representative at an electronics store, or most of my friends or family. Yet amazingly, it has been these very people that have helped me understand happiness the most.

This book is meant to offer a cathartic experience to us all, most of all me. Life may not be complicated, but it sure can be hard--really hard. The concepts included in these pages work for me because I have had to learn each of them painfully over the course of my 44 years. (Actually, by the time you read this, I may be 60-years-old. Writing books is also hard.) I didn't learn these concepts from a book, yet here I am writing a book now. Why? Because I don't want to forget these lessons; and maybe, just possibly, you have also learned these lessons and wish to not forget them either. We both know how easily, on occasion, we have forgotten lessons, and probably will again.

Therefore, since you and I are going to spend some time together, let me fill you in on who I am. What follows may indeed be far too thorough of a biography. I offer my story, however, as evidence that there is nothing incredibly unusual about me, which I believe proves that I am a credible source of information on the average person's pursuit of happiness. For any of you who feel uninterested in my short biography, I completely understand. If so, skip ahead to Chapter One. I won't take it personally.

LIFE BEYOND GREENUP

Greenup (pronounced like "throw-up," only green. It is comments like this that have rendered me unelectable as a candidate for mayor), where I'm from, is the largest town in the smallest county in Illinois. For as long as I can remember, 1600 people have resided there, at least that's what those green signs on each end of town say. I was born on May 23, 1961, in nearby Mattoon, since Greenup doesn't have a hospital. My youth was pretty typical of small-town America with baseball, bike riding, school, dogs, etc. Mom had a serious problem with drugs and alcohol while I grew up, which most definitely hurt our relationship and explains her curious and obvious absence in the stories that follow. She was a very good person; I just came along at a very bad time. Dad was a committed father, albeit a product of the emotional stoicism that accompanied rural mid-western men who survived the Depression. I can't tell you if my childhood was happy because I don't have a point of comparison. I can tell you, with some confidence, that my childhood preceded my adulthood, except on those often-repeated occasions when they seem to run parallel.

My earliest aspirations were to be a professional baseball player. I would have made it, too, had my career not been cut short at 20-years-old by a severe lack of talent. Like so many others, I was a good player for a small team in the middle of nowhere. I was perfect for the slow pitch softball leagues where the winning team gets the keg of beer (I know. I played softball for beer far too many years).

I did well in high school and my academic aptitude was one of my most marketable qualities early on. My senior year the University of Illinois awarded me a full scholarship that I didn't accept. I was in love. Lisa was the most beautiful girl in our senior class (a total of 76) and she liked *me*! The move to Champaign-Urbana, a 75-mile journey, would surely end our budding romance. I decided instead to commute to Eastern Illinois University for four years and pay for college myself. After graduating from college, however, Lisa left me. Bummer.

My original vocation was in radio and television. I started as a disc jockey while still in my teens and worked at the campus radio station in a variety of management positions. Eventually I got the chance to be a reporter and producer at the local CBS affiliate in Terre Haute, Indiana. It was a fabulous opportunity for a 21-year-old kid. After six months, I quit. Crazy.

After some odd (literally) jobs, I found myself in Chicago almost a year later. My sister, a wonderful human being with a propensity to worry, spearheaded a less-than-subtle campaign to salvage my life. (She's 17 years older than I am and a lifetime without children has left her with a huge and untapped maternal instinct.) With her support, I got a job with Marshall Field's in Chicago and an apartment complete with the type of roaches that only a large city can produce. I refer to this era as my Underwood Chicken Spread years. Other than the occasional frozen pizza, the only thing I ate was this curious, spam-like gelatinous mass--on white bread, of course.

I met Lori in 1984. We worked together. I told her she looked beautiful every day for a year. Literally.

"You look very nice today, Lori," says Dave shyly.

"Thanks," responds Lori, increasingly less amused.

Imagine a repeat of the above two lines every work day for one year.

I never asked her out.

A mutual friend became so frustrated by my snail-like dating strategy that she invited us both out on a double date with her boyfriend--three times. Our friend's efforts finally worked. Lori and I moved in with each other less than three months from our first date and were married one year later, the day after Valentine's Day, 1986.

Lori is the best thing that has ever happened to me. I know that sounds like the inside of a greeting card. Still, I mean it. This fun and charming woman has the most joyous spirit I have ever encountered. I love her more than life itself. I cry while watching bad romantic movies on planes because I think of my love for her. My guess is I fall right behind Lori's horses in her order of affection. That's very high.

In 1990, when Lori was eight months pregnant with our first child and I was a rising star in the Marshall Field's training and development department, we discovered that we were not happy. We had no time for each other, no time for ourselves, and no time for our new child on the way. I quit Marshall Field's and we moved down to Orlando, Florida: no job, no doctor, pregnant wife, and Goofus the dog. Stupid---me, not the dog. Okay, maybe both.

Brooke was born May 12, 1990. She is daddy's little girl--plays me like a fiddle and costs me a lot of money. I love her more than life itself. I know, more clichés. If you have kids, you know what I mean. She is smart, pretty, quickwitted, responsible, and impatient. Even as a teenager she has better judgement than me. I fall right behind her horse and the Internet in her order of affections. That's very high. Shortly after Brooke was born, I found a job in Orlando as a human resources manager for a hotel management company.

Slade was born in 1993. Man, is he good looking! Genetically, he is the best Lori and I can do. He is stubborn, funny, vain, kind, smart, offbeat, unfocused, sensitive, and loud. His room is a disaster area. He is a lot like me. We fight often, but, you got it, I love him more than life itself. I fall right behind any of his one thousand hot wheel cars in his order of affection. Oh, and his video games. Yes, that's very high.

When Slade was born, I was the Vice President of Human Resources and Quality for that hotel management company--an executive with responsibilities that included overseeing the PGA National Resort in Palm Beach Gardens,

Florida, the Lodge and Bath Club in Ponte Vedra Beach, the Buena Vista Palace Resort and Spa in Disney Village, and many more resort spas. A lot of people in my life thought this was the perfect job. Two years later I quit. Idiot.

After a couple of years starting up the Southeastern regional office for a human resources consulting firm, I committed myself to the Leadership Difference, an "enter-train-ment" company that I founded. Our mission is "Laugh and Learn!" Most of the next nearly ten years, which brings us to today, have exceeded all my preconceived notions of success. I have a family I love deeply, ample time to spend with my wife and children, a comfortable home, financial security, independence, and a carefree lifestyle. We moved to the mountains of Colorado where I hike a lot with Martini and Rossi (our two yellow labs, not the vermouth). We recently adopted Captain Morgan. Apparently, we are slowly accumulating a full canine liquor bar. Captain Morgan, or "Sparky" as we call him, is a kind soul with the wounded expression of someone who has witnessed great tragedy. Morgan survived Hurricane Katrina. Sadly, his owners did not.

Now you know a bit more about who you are dealing with. Keep in mind by the time this gets published, I might very well be running a wine store and doing volunteer work. Or not. Or part. Who knows? But one thing is for sure, it *has* been a life. It is a life that has held joy, heartache, anger, and angst--and that was just earlier today. Essentially, it is a life just like yours.

I will always remember something a friend, Dr. Steve Shealy, once said to me during one of my many moments of personal anguish: "Dave, act out of faith, not out of fear." Thanks, Steve.

Now, with a large amount of faith and a huge dose of fear, I present to you:

Live and Learn...or Die Stupid.

CHAPTER ONE

Be the Hand

INTERNAL LOCUS OF CONTROL

Being a speaker, trainer, and entertainer is an interesting profession. I spend a good deal of time loafing, at least when compared to my workload in the corporate world. Back then, I would work 50 to 60 hours a week and every moment I felt physically, mentally, and/or emotionally shackled to my job. Now, my cell door is open. Occasionally I have to step back inside: the conference call with a potential new client, talking with my accountant, filling out government paperwork, waiting out a travel delay. These are moments of incarceration. But for the most part, I loaf: sharing good times with my family, mountain biking and hiking, walking our dogs, listening to music, working out at the gym, reading, watching a movie, having a fine glass of wine, surfing the Internet. These are all examples of beautiful loafing for me.

Most of all, I love to spend time pondering. It has become my preferred loafing activity, alone or with a friend. I love to ponder, and I love to be paid to share my ponderings. This is my favorite thing: to amuse and lighten while I entertain and enlighten.

Often, after I speak, people come up to me and ask me whether I have a book. I have always been immensely flattered by this query. For the longest time I have said, "Oh, I'm just an average guy. Why in the world would you want to read a book that I wrote?" People have responded by saying how much they enjoyed listening to me, and how they would like to be able to revisit the concepts I presented when their memory of the event begins fading.

Consequently, after much hand wringing and self-talk, I have decided to write a book. This book will prove I am not a guru and, hopefully, establish more credibility for the concepts I have been offering. For me, it really isn't a book so much as it is a conversation between the two of us. The only thing, however, is I'm the one doing the talking, though in my mind I'm always remembering voices from hours of interactions with others (at least I'm hoping those voices in my head are from past conversations). What follows is a summation, of sorts, of all these previous conversations.

Okay, so we're just talking here, you and me. Let me ask you right off, do you think it is possible to be happy? I mean, really happy--not fake happy, not "I really have no reason to *not* be happy" or "I'm happy for the most part happy." I mean real contentment. I wonder. It seems to me that for a person to be consistently happy, content, and successful, he or she will need to possess certain characteristics. Maybe people just need some kind of a recipe or checklist for happiness.

Everything that is difficult in life--and I think "being happy" certainly qualifies as a challenge--starts with an instruction manual. This instruction manual, containing a checklist of characteristics of a happy person, is what

I have been pursuing my whole life. If we had such a list, we could develop our own little happiness curriculum around any characteristics that we don't currently possess. Or we could use the checklist to do diagnostic work when we are unhappy. Wouldn't that be cool? But what the heck would be on that checklist? Hmmm. I believe there is one fundamental attribute critical to our chances to be happy. Let's chat about that first.

"THEY WOULDN'T BE HAPPY IF YOU HUNG THEM WITH A NEW ROPE."

When I was 14-years-old, I started working for my dad each summer. He ran a little heating and air conditioning business in Greenup, Illinois. I would crawl around under houses or up in attics running duct-work to heat registers. Since he also sold and repaired appliances, I would also go along with him on deliveries or service calls. He paid me 25 cents an hour. (Did I mention that my father survived the Depression?) Anytime I would bring up my paltry compensation, I would be regaled for hours with stories of that era. Apparently my dad subsisted entirely on jam sandwiches ("That's two pieces of bread jammed together, Boy.") and entertained himself by riding a bicycle that he made himself. I never asked exactly how he managed this engineering feat for fear that I would be subjected to even more outrageous stories.

I was also responsible for keeping my dad's books. Now that I run my own business and have kids, I realize how questionable Dad's decision was to allow a 14-year-old to do his books. Anyway, while handling my dad's books, I began to realize some things about human nature. First of all, my father--a veteran of World War II, poverty, the Depression, and self -proclaimed "tough son of a bitch"--was a softie. With a struggling business his income was small, yet he always had a large amount of accounts receivable on the books. These were the people who had not yet paid Dad. Each month he would tell me to send out the statements, and each month I would dutifully go through these past due accounts and send out reminders. Over time, I knew who would actually pay and who wouldn't. Essentially, these accounts fell into four categories:

1. The people who had no money but would pay a little bit each month
2. The people who had no money and didn't pay at all
3. The people who had money but preferred to pay off their bill over time (since Dad didn't add interest)
4. The people who had money and didn't pay

My father had great admiration for the first group of people and continued to provide service for them, despite the fact that they owed him money. He groused quite a bit about the second group, but continued to provide them service when they needed it. ("Can't let 'em freeze to death, now can we, Boy?") Dad was most amused with the third group, often saying, "That's how they got rich."

For the final group my father had a special saying: "They wouldn't be happy if you hung them with a new rope." This he would say as he shook his head. My father had a lot of obtuse, vaguely violent little clichés like this. In fact, I am pretty sure that during my formative years, between the ages 12 and 16, my dad responded to every question I asked him with one of the following clichés:

"I used to complain about my shoes until I met the man with no feet."

"Stand up for yourself or you'll be knocked down by someone else."

"Eat well 'cause it may be your last meal."

"No need to be depressed, things will get worse."

"Don't believe anything you hear and only half of what you see. But if it stinks, it stinks."

"I'm not gonna chew your ass out. I'm gonna chew around it and let it fall out!"

And, of course: "They wouldn't be happy if you hung them with a new rope."

"What does THAT mean?" I would ask.

"Bitchers and belly-achers," he would respond. "Those people wouldn't know a happy thought if it bit them in the butt. Call and ask them why they haven't paid, and they'll give you a hundred reasons. Add a service charge to their account, and every damn one of 'em will call me a crook."

"Why would they call you a crook when it is their fault that they haven't paid?" I responded with the naiveté of a 14-year-old.

"That's just it. They won't see it as their fault. They will think they are the victim and then refuse to pay out of principle. They'd complain about a sunny day because the bright light hurts their eyes."

I didn't know it then, but I just got my first memorable lesson in the concept of *internal locus of control*.

WHEN YOUR CTL CONTAINER IS FULL

Years later, as my eleven year career in corporate human resources management was grinding to a halt, I spent a good part of my day listening to employee grievances. Some were very legitimate and others were not.

After listening endlessly to both categories, I stopped trying to distinguish between the two. I was just plain burned out. I had become a very directive counselor. I now feel badly for those employees who came to me during this time.

"Hey, Bob. How can I help you today?" I would ask as the meeting began with an unhappy employee.

"Mr. Mitchell, I requested next Tuesday off and my manager denied the request," said the obviously troubled Bob.

"Then quit, Bob," and with that I would stand and escort Bob back to the door.

Bob seemed unsatisfied with my employee relations skills. Clearly, it was time for me to find a new line of work. My CTL container was full.

The CTL container, by the way, is a rarely discussed but tremendously important part of your neurological function. You won't read about it in medical journals, but I am here to tell you that many of life's conflicts and your personal anguish are both directly related to the status of your CTL container.

You look puzzled. Oh, you've never heard of the CTL container? Well then, you probably don't know what CTL stands for.

Crap Tolerance Level.

And when your CTL container overflows, it is ugly. I mean UGLY!

It wasn't that I didn't care. I just got worn out dealing with the people who always had a problem. As a result, after 11 years I was unable to muster the strength to find out which person had a legitimate concern and who was just a bitcher and bellyacher. Like I said, my CTL container was full.

Saddest part of all, I was becoming a bitcher and bellyacher, too.

I resigned and started my own company.

Today, I laugh when people commend me for the confidence to start my own company. Confidence had nothing to do with it. I couldn't get out of bed and go face that job in human resources one more day. I started my own company out of desperation, not confidence.

I had no clients, no capital, no office, no sales experience, no presentations, and no clue. And, as I discovered when I took back the bill-paying responsibilities from my wife (my lovely wife, who I adore, but who has a fondness for credit limits), I had more debt than money.

I was happy as a lark. I had just received an advanced lesson on the power of *internal locus of control*.

LIFE IS A BALLOON

Few people really have a plan. Oh, we can make our lives make sense with some creative revisionist history, but the fact of the matter is most of us aren't operating with a master strategy. However, I do take some pride in the fact that I have been willing to make adjustments in my life when I am not happy. I don't know how I come by this characteristic, but I am sure my father's relentless sharing of Depression-era stories had some influence. I realize now that this may have been the greatest gift my father gave to me. Consequently, it is a gift that I try to share. It is the gift of internal locus of control. Like many concepts, internal locus of control is most easily explained using a metaphor.

When I do keynote speeches I "invite" four members of my audience to join me on stage. I say invite, although the correct verb would probably be coerce. Maybe threaten. Or humiliate. Anyway, I manage to get four people up there with me. These four people and a balloon are all I need to provide a great example of locus of control. Try it yourself at your next party.

Line the four people up parallel to each other and about six feet apart. Tell them that you are going to tap the balloon to the first person, who will then tap it to the second person, who will tap it to the third person, who will tap it to the fourth person who will reverse the action until the balloon returns to the starter. Tell them that at no time is the balloon allowed to touch the floor.

The floor is *baaaad*.

Begin. It won't be hard. I have done this exercise hundreds of times with all kinds of people and only one time did they fail. I think it was a bad balloon. The experience won't necessarily be pretty. The balloon will go every which way, and people will be lurching in the most awkward ways as they use their hands and any other available body parts to try to guide the balloon back in the direction it needs to go.

Now, insert the word life for balloon in this experience and you've got yourself a metaphor for locus of control. (Or is it an analogy? Allegory? I never was sure about the correct usage of those words. I'm sure Mrs. Jackson, my high school English teacher, just released a sigh of resignation somewhere.) Anyway, let me explain.

Imagine if there were a sliding scale within each of us that represents our locus of control. On one side of the sliding scale is an internal locus of control and on the other side is an external locus of control. Where would your setting be on a consistent basis? Where you are on the scale has a lot to do with your level of happiness and success. You see, if your setting is over toward the external locus of control, then you are like the balloon in the exercise. That is to say, you are at the mercy of the hands that smack you.

Those hands are life events. Each time you are smacked by a life event, you have no choice but to travel in that direction.

People with an external locus of control have a hard time remaining happy. They can, however, tell you why they aren't happy: "My boss is a jerk"; "My job sucks"; "My spouse is an idiot, but we stay together for the kids. We want to make sure they are just as miserable as we are." These are the people that my father said would not be happy if you hung them with a new rope. They cannot achieve happiness because the key to their happiness exists outside of themselves.

This is exactly why so many of the people I counseled came back to my office again and again while I was a human resources manager. They were victims. Every time life got a little off track, they found something or someone else to blame. Unfortunately, toward the end of my career in corporate human resources, my own sliding scale of locus of control landed firmly on the external side as well.

People with an internal locus of control are like the hands that swat the balloon. They evaluate the developments in their lives and smack them in the direction they want their lives to go. It may not turn out exactly as they plan, but the fact that they take an active role in guiding their life means that it generally heads in the right direction. That is why I felt so much more happiness when I DECIDED, when I TOOK ACTION, when I walked out of the unhappy situation I was in while in the corporate world. Now, understand that I had been planning my business for a year, but it was more fantasy than reality. When I committed to a new life direction, I batted the balloon in the direction that I wanted it to go.

Now, reality check! I still have moments...days...even a week of unhappiness here and there. Slow business, bad luck, no mojo--I can end up in a funk for whatever reason. Knowing what it takes to be happy is a lot easier than executing it. I will tell you that there are a few things that can pull me out of these states. A paycheck in the mail always works like a charm. Someone might call and hire me; something randomly positive might occur like an email from a friend or a positive and reinforcing letter from a client; my mojo might mysteriously reappear (don't worry, we'll discuss mojo in chapter seven). All of these are frighteningly unpredictable. Or, I can sit down and decide what I need to do--what I NEED TO DO--to make things better. Inevitably, all it takes to begin feeling better is the latter. It just seems to take me a while to figure that out.

Looking back, many of the clichés my father shared with me involved this concept, "If you can change it, change it." That's a direct reference to using an *internal locus of control*. "Do something, even if it's wrong." He always said this when he knew I was agonizing over a situation, or if I was bummed out because of boredom.

While I don't encourage people to be impulsive and perhaps multiply their troubles, I do think that inaction is far more dangerous than taking the wrong action. It seems as though it is easier to know what to do if you realize that what you are doing is wrong, than it is to sit around and do nothing besides try to figure out what's going on. I think it is kind of like the kid's game where a person hides something, then as the seekers search for the item, the person tells the seekers if they are getting warmer or colder depending on how close or far they are from the item. If there were another player who just stayed in one place and guessed where the item was, my bet is that he or she would take much longer to find the item. Maybe that's just me.

Another thing about locus of control, it's situational. By that I mean that a person can possess an internal locus of control about virtually every element of his or her life, but externalize control over just one thing, like a relationship with a parent, spouse, child, boss, colleague, or subordinate. I know when I start getting stressed out, it's usually a result of my feeling like a victim to something within my own life. So next time you are out of sorts, check to see if you have externalized the locus of control in some aspect of your life.

Not happy? What are you doing about it? People with an internal locus of control get bummed, too. It's just that they take action quickly to fix it. They are the hands, not the balloon. I don't believe that happy people have a great plan, or that they have been more fortunate than the rest of us. I believe their happiness has more to do with their *internal locus of control*. If life is a balloon…

Be the hand!

Oh, and on second thought, don't do that balloon exercise at your next party. You'll look like a dork.

CHAPTER TWO

My Own Private Idaho

TRANSITIONARY SPACE

You know, it occurs to me that before we go too far here I need to share my theory on reality. Actually, I doubt it is my own theory. I am sure many people, far brighter than I am, have written volumes on the nebulous nature of human reality. Of course, I do not read so I am unaware of this research. Well, to be fair, I do read some. While on airplanes I read *Esquire Magazine*. I also read *GQ, Details, Men's Health, Men's Fitness, The Sporting News, Wine Spectator, Wine Enthusiast, Sports Illustrated, Rolling Stone, Blender, Spin, MOJO, Men's Journal, No Depression* (it's about music, don't worry) and *New York Mets Inside Pitch*. Sometimes, when I am desperate for reading material, I will sink to *Psychology Today* or *Scientific American* or some such thing. They are kind of dry though. No celebrity pictures either.

Anyway, I do read, but not really what one might call "meaningful literature." So I am sure my theory on **transitionary space** is not new. But it was new to me, and as always, the result of obsessive pondering. Here's how I imagine human reality working. I believe that all of us human types who possess fully functioning (or as is the case with me and my eyeglasses, artificially corrected) sensory receptors (you know: eyes, ears, nose, mouth, nerve-endings), essentially have access to the same data that surrounds us. I call this entire database of information that is collectible by human sensory receptors **absolute human reality**. *Absolute human reality* is potentially the same for all people. To make this seem formal and important, I will repeat the definition in a separate font:

> *ABSOLUTE HUMAN REALITY* IS THE SUM TOTAL OF ALL DATA THAT CAN BE PERCEIVED BY HUMAN BEINGS USING THEIR SENSORY RECEPTORS: VISION, HEARING, SMELL, TASTE AND TOUCH. IT IS THE SAME FOR ALL HUMANS.

Of course, for us--and by us I mean all human beings--to experience the same *absolute human reality* we would all have to be standing in the same spot, facing the same direction, with the same acuity in all five senses, with...well, you get the idea. Obviously each individual's ability to experience *absolute human reality* is limited by his or her physical setting.

Additionally, I believe our sensory receptors are far better at collecting data than the cognitive function of the brain is at processing that data. In other words, we are immersed in far more gathered information than we actually choose to use. Basically, I believe we operate in spite of a serious design flaw. For human beings, input exceeds capacity to process. I mean, don't we all choose to only focus on certain things even though we are seeing or hearing much more? I know my wife has accused me of hearing the football score of the Minnesota Vikings amidst the swirling chaos of our household without hearing nary a word about my negligent household responsibilities. This is really just a self-preservation process to protect ourselves from being overwhelmed, or in my example above, to avoid doing the dishes and making coffee. Anyway, if we are collecting more data than we can process, then we must funnel, focus, and filter out certain information.

I consider the place within our minds where we select certain elements of *absolute human reality* and discard other elements to be our *transitionary space*. The end product of all this data collected from *absolute human reality* by our sensory receptors and shoved through our personal *transitionary space* is what I call **individual interpreted reality**.

Individual interpreted reality is the unique life journey that each person experiences. It is what guides a person's actions, forms his or her opinions, and either contributes to or subtracts from his or her consistent happiness. It explains each person's behaviors. For the married women reading this book, this might explain some of your husband's behaviors. I mean, how many times have you reacted to your husband's behavior with, "Why in the world would you do that?"

The answer is, "They are not IN your world!" Your husband's behavior made perfect sense in his world. Going to Hooter's to celebrate your anniversary was totally logical. Food's good, game's on, beer's cold....come on!

Anyway, as my dad used to say, let me draw you a $%&@-ing picture. Dad came to profanity late in life and reveled in the rebellious nature of its use.

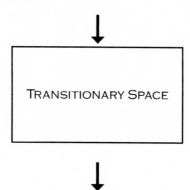

ABSOLUTE HUMAN REALITY

TRANSITIONARY SPACE

INDIVIDUAL INTERPRETED REALITY

So, if you assume (as I do) that each person constructs his or her individually interpreted reality with subsequent behaviors and happiness resulting from this construction, then one must examine the elements of the human condition that reside within transitionary space, since it is within transitionary space that *absolute human reality* (where everything is the same from human to human) is transformed into *individual interpreted reality* (where everything is unique to the individual).

Did anyone follow that? Whew! I think I have pretty much forfeited any chance of getting hired to write instructional manuals after that last paragraph.

Bottom line, I believe that there are some very important processes taking place within *transitionary space* that influence our happiness. Locus of control, from the last chapter, for instance, is one of these processes. The following chapters describe more. So, what should the reader take away from this discussion of how people construct reality? Probably a headache. But also, perhaps an appreciation that each of us has more influence over our life experience than we are conscious of. Perhaps by being more aware of how our approach to life influences our happiness, we can choose to do things that increase the quality of our life experience. Oh no, I'm beginning to sound like Tony Robbins. Not that there is anything wrong with Tony. He seems like a real confident guy. Walks on hot coals. Owns an island, I hear. Wow, I suck.

You know, let's just move on to self-loathing...er...I mean self-talk...the subject of our next chapter.

CHAPTER THREE

Buckaroo Banzai in Belize

POSITIVE SELF-TALK

I talk to myself.

You talk to yourself.

Everybody talks to themselves.

My wife talks to herself out loud, and when I catch her she says she is talking to our dogs (as if this were more reasonable).

I don't think there is anything more mysterious than our own brain. Our brain is so complicated that whole parts seem to work independently from one another. Performance psychologists talk about how positive visualization actually affects our physiology. In essence, our bodies are responding to an imagined scenario as if it were a real situation.

It makes perfect sense. I know I have conjured up negative imagery that resulted in a definite physiological response--a very unappealing response.

When I was in my early to mid-twenties, I worked hard to get established in the corporate world. I started my human resources career as a store trainer for Marshall Field's. I had no background in training and development and was (and still am) a bit of an introvert. While I knew I was a good and entertaining classroom instructor (a rare acknowledgement of my own value), I still felt a bit overwhelmed by other aspects of my job. Twelve to fourteen hour work days were the norm and each evening I would analyze upcoming challenges. This analysis would often have a negative tenor. I would worry about how to handle these situations and imagine that each challenge might be my demise.

Every three weeks or so I would experience intensely painful intestinal cramps.

I mean intensely painful.

I have had two kidney stones. They hurt. I mean, passing a rock through your...well, you get the picture. These intestinal cramps hurt even more.

I have had two children. Granted, the labor that accompanied their birth was far more painful for my wife than for me. Still, the pain I felt from my sense of helplessness while watching her labor was intense. The helplessness I felt from these intestinal cramps hit me even harder than the helplessness I experienced during Lori's labor.

I felt like that astronaut in the movie *Alien* who was the vessel from which the creature bursts forth. Each time it happened, I was pretty sure I was giving birth to an alien, and nothing gets your attention like giving birth to an alien.

The cramps would go on for hours and I would find myself lying on the floor of my bathroom, in the fetal position, praying for resolution. For three years I tried to draw correlations to certain foods. I monitored every possible variable I could think of. Finally, after three years of consistent, intermittent episodes of intense eye popping, excruciating pain, I decided to take extreme measures.

I went to a doctor.

Shocking.

Shocking for a man. After three years of pain and my wife's insistence, I yielded. I succumbed. I went to a doctor.

Seeing a doctor is very hard for many men. At 25-years-old I was not likely to receive the dreaded digital rectal exam, the most daunting deterrent to any visit to the doctor. In fact, at 25 I didn't even know what a digital rectal exam was. Now, at 44, I know. Maybe this is why I choose female doctors. Smaller digits.

What I did get to experience at 25 was the GI. I still don't know what that means. All I know is they have upper GIs, lower GIs, diagonal GIs, "bend over let me introduce you to a" GI. They have all sorts of GIs. I got to experience all of them and I am here to tell you, ain't none of them pleasant.

It's particularly confusing when a smiling doctor, barely able to contain his or her glee, tells you, "You're fine."

What?

Does that mean that everyone has excruciating abdominal cramps every three or four weeks? Ladies, put down your hands.

Okay, so roughly half of the population might have cramps like these, but I am not part of that demographic.

So, confirming what I had maintained all along, the visit to the doctor had accomplished nothing. Nothing except educate me on the humiliation of the GI procedure. Three weeks after my visit to the doctor I was back on the floor of my bathroom in the fetal position begging for resolution.

Back to the doctor. A different doctor. One with a different approach. No GIs. Hardly any discussion of my digestive tract at all. No, this doctor, an older man with a reassuring resemblance to Marcus Welby, asked me questions about my approach to life, not my diet. Then he said something that would change my life forever.

He told me my problem was in my head.

I hit him.

Okay, I didn't really hit him, but I've got to tell you, don't tell a Midwestern man, the product of an agricultural community, son of a Depression-era survivor, that he has a head problem. I bowed up. I went DeNiro on him. I said, "Oh no, Doc, I got pain. Pain YOU couldn't handle!"

"I know," he said, "and the origin of that pain is a result of how you are approaching your life mentally." He went on to explain that my body was responding to the mental stress to which it was being subjected, stress that I was creating: the endless analysis, negative speculation, and conjecture, the obsessing--all of these issues were creating an environment containing such duress that my intestines rebelled. Essentially, he summarized the psychology of all this with one sentence: "You have a third party relationship with yourself and that third party is way too critical."

In a nutshell, he explained, the way I was talking to myself was affecting my physical health and happiness. The cognitive function of my brain was influencing the autonomous function of my brain.

I was worrying myself sick.

Almost immediately the intestinal cramps started to subside. Now that I knew that they were self-inflicted I started to manage them. But that was just the tip of the iceberg. I began to realize how many other aspects of my emotional, mental, spiritual, and even (pause for effect) *physical* well-being were being affected by my negative self-talk. Of course, realizing something and changing something are two entirely different exercises.

Years passed before the next epiphany.

YOUR BEST FRIEND IS NOT ALWAYS THERE FOR YOU

Let me ask you this. Do you have a best friend? If you don't, lie. It is very depressing to admit to yourself that you don't have a best friend.

You may have more than one. I have two: my wife and Jerry Herships. My wife has shared virtually every important event in my life for the last 20 years. She has seen me at my best and my worst. Her devotion and support has always been unwavering. Her love is unconditional, as is my love for her.

Jerry is an entertainer and seminary student (It's complicated!) and the similarity in our vocations has provided the foundation of our relationship. We often work together. The shared experiences and the fact that we think alike, laugh about the same things, and have similar values have all helped forge our special bond.

My two best friends are not the same two that I have had my entire life. I have had two other best friends. Dennis Rodebaugh held the title from ages four to twenty-one. I lost track of Dennis over the years. I think of him a lot, but our lives have grown too far apart for us to be best friends. However, he recently came to visit and I remembered quickly why he had been my best childhood friend.

Scott Shafer has been akin to the utility infielder of best friends. He has always been in my life and every now and then steps back into the role. However, the distance between us and the passing of time has largely regulated Scott to the friendship bench. That's not a bad thing. It allows me the benefit of friendship "depth."

Anyway, my point is that I have two best friends. I bet most of you have at least one close friend. While it is unlikely that I know this person, I bet I can describe your relationship with him or her. You feel most comfortable with this person. You don't try to be something that you are not. You know that he or she loves you for who you are, warts and all. It is this comfort-level and unconditional love that makes the relationship so special. You may have grown up with this person, you may be related, you may even be married, but one thing is for sure: you love him or her simply for the person he or she is and vice-versa.

Well, let me tell you a few things about your best friend.

He or she is not always there for you.

He or she is probably not with you right now as you read this. He or she probably isn't with you at work. He or she isn't with you when you take your shower.

Not every shower. Okay, I'm guessing.

The fact is, no matter how close you are with your best friend, you will spend more of your life without that person than with him or her. You can marry this person or go into business with him or her, yet you will still experience more of life alone than with this person. There is only one person who will experience every life event with you. In other words, there is only one person who will always be there for you.

You.

You will spend your whole life with you. Because of this odd third party relationship between the cognitive you and the physical you, it is as if there are two distinct entities residing in your body.

You know what that means don't you? You better like you. You see, you can get rid of everybody else in your life. If you don't like your wife, divorce her. There are other fish in the sea. Kids are monsters? Give 'em up for adoption. Some loving family will take a chance on them. Boss is a jerk? Just walk into his or her office and say, "You know what (insert boss' name)? Later days and holidays!" Then turn and with your best cocky strut say, "Let me give you the last view of me you're ever gonna get."

For additional effect you can add some smack talk that I learned from my daughter, Brooke. Look your boss directly in the eye and recite, "Loser, loser, double loser, as if... whatever. Get the picture, duh?" To actually be effective you must accompany this smack talk with the corresponding choreography of hand gestures, head tilts, and swiveling hips. Ask any teenager to teach you.

You can get rid of everyone in your life if you don't like the way they treat you. You can get on a plane and fly to Belize. When you get to Belize, rent a bike. Ride that bike to the beach. Drop the bike and run. Run like the wind down that beach until you reach one of the most secluded spots in the entire world. There is not another human being within miles of you. But remember this.

"No matter where you go, there you are." (from *Buckaroo Banzai and the Adventures of the Eighth Dimension.* A great, obscure science-fiction movie.)

You can't run from you. To sum up, if you plan to achieve happiness, you better start with the relationship you have with yourself.

Having said that, most of us have a tenuous relationship at best with ourselves. If you are like me, you get tired of yourself. I mean, come on. Every single moment of every single day spent with me? I am 44 years old.

I don't think that's old, but it is the oldest I have ever been. Forty-four years spent entirely with myself. It is exhausting! Do you know we have never taken separate vacations! We haven't so much as had dinner apart during that time. Even when I try to take a quick break from me, boom, there I am. I get sick of me!

The worst moment often is first thing in the morning. You know what I mean? You get out of the bed and you go to the bathroom. And there's the mirror.

Who started that? Why is there a mirror in the bathroom? That is such a bad idea. Who was the freak that thought we needed a mirror to watch what happens in a bathroom?

Anyway, you start your day by catching a glimpse of yourself in the mirror. You stare at your image. This is definitely not the best you are going to look today. You stare and say to yourself, "Man, are you ugly!"

"But that's okay, cause you're fat, too"

"Fat and ugly. I'll just call you 'Fugly'. Fat and ugly."

There it is: your morning motivational speech. Could you imagine if your boss met you at the door of your employment each morning and said, "Hey, Fugly's here. Let's get to work, Fugly! Let's close some deals, FUGLY." That would be pretty hard to take. It certainly wouldn't be inspiring. It definitely wouldn't build self-esteem and confidence. But at least you could quit your job. Unfortunately, however, you can't leave *you*.

Now I am not suggesting that you get up each morning, lick your finger, place it on your hip, and listen for the sizzle as you look at yourself in the mirror and exclaim, "Oh, my God. You are sooo GORGEOUS!"

It may work for George Clooney, but it doesn't work for the rest of us.

My point is if each of us had the same relationship with ourselves as we do with our best friend, imagine how much happier we would be. Our best friend knows we are not perfect and they love us anyway. That's because they define us by our good qualities, not by our flaws. Oh sure, they support us as we try to improve and remind us when we fall short of our potential, but ultimately they love us unconditionally.

Human beings are not capable of perfection. If this is your goal, you are in for a lifetime of disappointment. The funny thing is that I have met some people in my time that appear to believe they have achieved perfection. They are annoying. The fact that they are annoying makes them imperfect. You see, perfection is impossible.

I remember coming home from school when I was 16-years-old. I was bummed because the most spectacular girl in school, who I dug like a ditch, wouldn't spit on the best part of me. The pain of our unrequited love radiated through my entire being such that even my dad, with his limited emotional sensitivity, could see that I was depressed.

"What's wrong with you?" Dad asked.

Hesitantly, I offered the reason from my morose state. "There's this girl at school that I really, really like but she doesn't like me. I think it's my nose." I have one of those long, thin Romanesque-sort-of-noses that look fabulous on Matt Lauer and Adrian Brody. I didn't like it on me.

"Yeah, you got a big nose," Dad said in a matter of fact way.

It was at this moment that I realized that my nurturing needs in life would be fulfilled by people other than my father.

Dad quickly realized that his response had not brightened my spirits. "Well, I mean, Son, your nose is right there on your face so we've all seen it. What makes you think this girl doesn't like you because of your nose?"

"Well, sometimes kids have pointed out that I have a big nose, so I just assume if this girl doesn't like me, it's cause of my nose."

And then Dad offered what appeared to be an early indication of dementia. "Listen, the only kids pointing out your nose are the ones with big ears."

cricket sounds

"What?"

"Son, everyone has flaws. Some flaws you can see, others you can't-- and thems the ones you should worry about. Anyway, if someone is pointing out your flaws, it's because they don't want anyone seeing theirs. That's all. And if that girl don't like you for something as stupid as the size of your nose, then she ain't worth ruining your day over."

I tell you, I heard what my dad said and immediately--within 10 years--I got it. Like most 16-year-olds, I was somewhat slow on the uptake. But eventually I realized that we all magnify our own imperfections because we are so doggone familiar with them. The key is not the fact that we have flaws. Our gifts are the key.

How do you nurture the relationship you have with yourself? I think you start by listening to your self-talk. Do you talk to yourself the way you would expect your best friend to talk to you? Do you define yourself by your positive qualities while striving to be the best person you can be? I think that's the goal.

Positive self-talk.

By the way, my dad ended our little counseling session with this nugget, "And, by the way, ain't nothing wrong with your nose."

I remember feeling like my dad had told me he loved me for the very first time. A few years later I would meet Lori. She loves my nose. Dad was right.

CHAPTER FOUR

Hats in the Highway

POSITIVE FOCUS

I must admit that I am a bit cynical. I don't read self-help books because I tend to dismiss their advice as overly-simple and Pollyanna-ish. As a result, it makes perfect sense that I would write a book that examines the personal characteristics that promote a happy and contented life using research culled only from my musings. Perhaps that is why I have struggled to write this book for so long.

One example of my misguided disdain for self-help literature revolves around *The Power of Positive Thinking* by Norman Vincent Peale--an undisputable classic in providing a framework for a happier existence written by a hugely intelligent and insightful spiritual leader. I, of course, dismissed it as syrupy optimism after having read it in my mid-30s. It would be several years later when the memories of my first child's birth and a friend's baseball hat collection would lead me to rethink the impact one's perspective has on one's life.

Babies are lazy

My wife and I made a decision to wait five years after we were wed before we started a family. It is probably the only example of a plan we have ever had during our marriage. We generally...no, we are always impulsive in our major life decisions. So the fact that we decided to wait five years to have our first child and actually made it four and a half years is the best example we can offer for having a plan. Therefore Brooke, our daughter and first-born, was planned.

As is so often the case with first-time parents, we read every book about parenthood and pregnancy. We gleefully prepared for the new arrival, painting and purchasing and outfitting and generally engaging in the rampant materialism that accompanies the birth of a child. Entire evenings and social gatherings would revolve around a shift or a kick by the baby. We would invite family, friends, UPS delivery people, and street musicians to feel my wife's stomach. We learned the language of the fertile: trimester, contraction, Lamaze, and sonogram.

Nine months of unbridled anticipation came to fruition on May 12, 1990, when my wife gave birth to our baby girl. Then, when we brought our bundle of joy home, I was overwhelmed with one singular feeling.

Disappointment.

Yep.

Babies are lazy.

Brooke was a healthy, normal, beautiful baby. Healthy, normal, beautiful babies don't do much. They don't engage you in interesting conversation. They don't generate revenue for the household. They don't help with chores. And they don't play catch.

That is when I realized my desire for fatherhood, planned as it might have been, was rooted in a desire to have someone to play catch with. Brooke, the baby, didn't play catch. Heck, she didn't even walk! In fact, she not only didn't walk, but she showed no interest in walking. How could this be, I asked myself? Walking would be so useful to her, especially until she gets a driver's license.

That's when I started reading Herzog.

I probably picked up the book thinking it was the memoirs of Whitey Herzog, the major league baseball manager.

But this Herzog was an educational theorist. I was already hooked before I realized this guy wasn't talking baseball. When I read Herzog's theory about the steps involved in learning, I realized that Brooke's situation went *beyond* not knowing how to walk. Brooke suffered from what Herzog referred to as unconscious incompetence.

She didn't know she didn't know how to walk. My daughter was clueless.

Soon Brooke became aware she didn't know how to walk. You could see her eyes follow you as you moved swiftly around the room while upright on your legs. You could tell she was curious about this fascinating skill.

At that point she had moved to Herzog's next level of learning: conscious incompetence. Arguably the most important step, Brooke had identified a skill that existed but that she did not possess, which would now allow her to go about learning that skill. She now knew she didn't know how to walk. In other words, she had gone from clueless to stupid.

Within months she had moved to <u>conscious competence</u> (she knew that she knew how to walk). You know, the stage during which the child selects the sharpest, most dangerous piece of furniture in your home and tries to walk toward it. The child teeters and staggers while steadily moving closer and closer to the corner of the coffee table that is exactly the same height as their right eye. She had gone from clueless to stupid to awkward.

Anyway, reaching this third stage is critical to expanding one's mind and skills. Or becoming a pirate named Lefty.

I feel compelled to offer an aside here to all you new and future parents: Why is it that we adults feel it necessary to assist our young toddlers in their quest to walk by grabbing their arms and holding them over their head? The only devices at their disposal to help them maintain balance--the arms--and we, the trusted caregivers, render them useless. I am convinced that all children would be walking at four months if their parents would stay out of the experience.

Now, back to Brooke. She would eventually become so adept at walking that she qualified as being <u>unconsciously competent</u>. She, like most of us, no longer had to think about walking. This is the state that most of us experience when we are walking--unless you close the local bar on a Saturday night, in which case you slide back to the conscious competence stage. Or sometimes just the unconscious stage--ba-da-boom! (Pause for reader to get the joke or reread as necessary.)

Brooke had moved from clueless to stupid to awkward to skilled.

While watching my daughter work her way through these steps, I was simultaneously experiencing one of my infrequent but life-altering epiphanies.

How much information exists in the world that I am completely unaware of? An even deeper thought followed that question: How much information exists in the world that I am incapable of being aware of?

Scooby-Doo moment....aaahuuuhh?

THERE IS NO REALITY

Like all human beings, I am self-centered. Unless you are Shirley MacLaine and have frequent-out-of body experiences, most of us spend our entire lives with one distinct point of view, our own. This point-of-view is limited by our own biomechanics. As fully functional human beings, we are capable of collecting data about reality using five sensory receptors: vision, hearing, smell, taste, and touch. In fact, we talked about this earlier when we discussed *individual interpreted reality*. We know, scientifically, that there are data, substances, entities, et cetera that we are unable to collect based on our biomechanical limitations. Therefore, some of this information is collected through scientific means (microscopes, Geiger counters, gas detectors, et al.) because at some point we were able to reach conscious incompetence and design technology to help us detect and understand things we were becoming aware of, but had little knowledge about.

What about the information that resides in that area of unconscious incompetence? I imagine that there is nearly an infinite amount of information about which we are clueless. Judging by the rapidity of change in the modern world, we have just scratched the surface of what we can know as human beings. That doesn't even speak to all the information we are just not capable of understanding due to the limitations of the human condition. Bottom line, the **absolute human reality** that I defined earlier is a tiny subset of all things that exist.

Whoa!

So for me, watching my daughter learn to walk became an exercise in quantum physics, biomechanics, and existential philosophy. (My wife says I think too much. I wonder what she means by that?)

What does this have to do with happiness? Well, I'm getting there. We still have to talk about baseball hats. Suffice it to say, when you realize that the version of reality you are working with is actually a subset of all that is real, that can give you pause for thought. It opens up the possibility of alternative realities. That said, you may well be wondering (or pondering), what good are alternative realities when they reside beyond the scope of the human condition? Good question, and that is where the story about baseball hats get introduced.

IT MUST BE SOME ODD STATE LAW IN TEXAS

I have a friend who is a behavioral psychologist. Actually, I have two friends who are psychologists. The fact that pyschologists keep entering my life randomly may be a compelling hint from the universe about my need for therapy! Anyway, they are both odd--not in a weird way, but in that endearing, eccentric way. The two of them provide great fodder for conversation, both because of their knowledge *and* their behavior.

Tom, one of these friends, lives in Texas. He collects baseball hats-- major league baseball hats. Because he was aware of my love of the game (I played organized baseball until the age of 20 and would later be revered as a successful coach at the tee-ball level), Tom felt that I would appreciate his collection of hats. I didn't have the heart to tell Tom that my love of baseball had very little to do with the apparel. On one of my trips to Texas, Tom invited me to his home to view his collection. As I stepped through the French doors and entered his den, I was surrounded by 125 major league baseball hats on display.

I don't think I could effectively paint a mental image for you of the enormity of a 125 major league baseball hat collection. But despite its enormity, it was not the size of the collection that was so awe-inspiring. It was the actual condition of these hats.

These were the nastiest, gnarliest hats I had ever seen. I mean, having played baseball I know how superstitious baseball players can be. When they go on a hitting streak, they don't change any articles of clothing, least of all their hats. But I am telling you, you cannot do what had been done to these hats on the baseball diamond. As I stood there in that doorway, dumbfounded, I tried to work up all the tact and diplomacy that my 11 years of corporate human resources training had afforded me before I turned to Tom.

"Dude, what's up with these hats? They are ugly!"

Yet another example of why I was not cut out for the corporate world.

"Oh, I forgot to tell you how I come by these hats," Tom replied. "I don't buy them. They are not given to me. I find them. I pick them up on interstate highways while riding my motorcycle."

Silence.

I remember thinking to myself, How long have I known Tom? How did I end up here in his home, alone? Does anyone know I am here?

Finally, I broke the awkward moment. "So, you found these hats on the road?"

"No, not roads. Not city streets or U.S. highways. It has to be an Interstate," corrected Tom. "And I have to be on my motorcycle." Tom was becoming increasingly manic.

"How long you been doing this, Tom?"

"About three years."

"THREE YEARS! And you have found 125 hats?"

"Well, probably more like 150, but a few have been so beat up that my wife wouldn't let me keep them."

Based on the condition of the "keepers," I imagined what the 25 rejects must have looked like. I also speculated on my wife's reaction to me collecting beat-up baseball hats and quickly realized that Tom's wife was either a saint or catatonic. Or both. Then it hit me.

This man had found an average of one major league baseball hat each week for the last three years while riding his motorcycle on interstate highways.

I could not recall seeing any hats on any road while riding in or on any vehicle in the entire 36 years that I had been on the planet up to that time. Yet this man was finding one hat a week of a specific type on a specific roadway while riding a specific vehicle.

I HAVE seen some shoes in the road.

Weird. Always a big clunky work-boot. Left foot. What's up with that? Are certain people driving to work with their window down and a boot just blows off their left foot? "Damn, I just lost my boot!"

Anyway, here I was, 36 years old with no hats. Then things got even more strange. That weekend, Tom took me to Galveston. It's about a two-hour drive to Galveston from Tom's house. On the way, he pointed out three hats. We weren't on an interstate highway, nor were we on his motorcycle, so we didn't stop to determine if they were major league baseball hats. But the fact that the man could point out three hats on the road to me in two hours, after I had gone 36 years without seeing one, was freaking me out.

Initially I figured it must be a Texas thang. I speculated that Texas must have some odd state law that requires that its residents celebrate each new day by flinging a hat out the window of their car. "Yeehaw, it's Wednesday!" I don't know; I've never lived in Texas.

When I returned home to Orlando, what do you think I saw?

Hats. Everywhere.

It was like an X-Files episode. You go your whole life without seeing a hat in the road and then someone comes up to you and says, "Oh, they're out there," and boom, there they are. Now I was really freaking out!

What's that about?

So I did a little research. That's generally how thorough I am. I do a little research, a little more observation, and a lot of pondering. I prefer to spend endless hours theorizing and hypothesizing on issues that have long ago been completely fleshed-out, meaning the mental mystery in which I am immersed is only a Google away from being solved. As a result, based on a smattering of actual science, here's what I think is going on here.

Our brains are struggling to make things simple enough for our mind to comprehend. This means that within our *transitionary space*, collected data is filtered for familiar information. We, in fact, have filters that ensure we notice (and place in our individual interpreted reality) information that is important to us. Some of this activity is done consciously; some of it is not.

We can see a lot more information than we can effectively process. In other words, the brain can collect far more visual information than the mind can process. As a result, we choose a focus. This can be a very conscious act. This focus now defines our visual information. For example, as a public speaker, when I look into my audience, I can choose the faces on which I will focus. If I choose to focus on someone who is smiling and nodding and laughing, then I will feel encouraged because my visual information seems to indicate that I am doing a great job. If I choose to focus on someone who has a furrowed brow and a scowl on their face, I will feel self-conscious and think I am not doing well.

Note to self and other speakers: The smiling, nodding, laughing person may be thinking, "What an idiot!" while the person scowling may be thinking, "This is the best information I have heard in my life!" You never know. That's why it's called individual INTERPRETED reality.

The fact is that I am changing my reality by what I choose to focus on. For further study on this subject, please reread Chapter Two, My Own Private Idaho, which introduces **individual interpreted reality** in this very book. (I know, I don't like to actually get up from the couch to do research, so I figured I would just reference my own book. Sweet, huh?)

It doesn't end there. In addition to the focus that you choose, there are also filters of which you are less conscious. Filters are little files that your brain sets up to protect you in the event that you choose the wrong focus. Let me give you an example. I love sports. If I am walking around the planet and sports information enters my field of view (swoosh), I will immediately notice it regardless of my current focus. I love music. Should music information enter my field of view, my brain will immediately (swoosh) change my focus to the music. I also love wine. When information about good wine enters my field of view, I will notice it. (Did I mention I am a certified sommelier? No real reason to mention that except for my need to brag about it, and my wanting you to understand a bit more about my love of wines.) I have other filters as well, but I am not going to share them all with you. You have a lot of filters, too.

The end result of all this is that our view of reality at any given time is largely determined by our focus and filters. For example, there are no two people closer than Lori and I are to one another. We have been together for nearly half of our lives, know each others' thoughts, and have many shared experiences. Yet when we go to the mall, despite the fact that we can be side-by-side, hand-in-hand, we are *not* in the same mall. My mall is comprised of music stores and sporting goods stores. Her mall is one big shoe store. Different focuses and different filters.

Tom had a baseball hat filter. For a couple of weeks, so did I. I dumped mine. I don't want to see hats in the road.

Having experienced the power of focus and filters, I now had a new perspective on Normal Vincent Peale's book. What at one time appeared to be misguided optimism and Pollyanna-ism, could now be viewed as choosing a positive focus. I realized that to choose to define reality in negative terms was not only self-destructive, but downright stupid. Who the heck wants to live in a world full of problems, barriers, and enemies, when a person can just as easily choose to live in a world of opportunity, resources, and friends?

I also began to better understand those people who constantly complained. I had wasted my time and theirs trying to impose my focus on them. My version of the world was accurate, but so was their version. That's why they seemed stubborn. They weren't stubborn, they were right. And so was I. The difference was that we each chose to focus on different elements of our world. I saw more of the good; they saw more of the bad.

Oh, don't get me wrong. I know there is evil in the world. I know bad things happen. The point is, how we choose to define the world and the people and the situations around us determines whether the world seems good or bad. **Absolute human reality** is neither good or bad--it is **individual interpreted reality** that takes on this dimension. Do we look for what is wrong or do we look for what is right? People who choose a positive focus have much less stress in their lives. People who choose a positive focus have an easier time being happy on a more consistent basis.

The choice seems clear...a positive focus. We are all delusional. Why not create a good delusion?

CHAPTER FIVE

Stunned by the Lollipop Guild

PROMOTE *SEAMWORK*

It had been quite a week.

Seven years ago my career as a public speaker/enter-trainer was chugging along at less than a breakneck pace. Although it was supporting us and I was pleased, I was still in a general state of anxiety about our future most of the time. But there was one week that was the most incredible week of my professional career.

On Monday I was in Basking Ridge, New Jersey doing some work for AT&T. On Tuesday, I was in Michigan speaking to General Electric. On Wednesday, I was in Virginia in front of the CIA. (Okay, so it was the human resources department, but it is still cool to say that I was speaking to the CIA. I remember being very apprehensive about that gig. What happens if they are not satisfied? I have heard stories.)

Each of the above clients had hired me to do a team-building event. During each of these events I used an exercise I creatively referred to as the rope exercise. I called it this because it involved a rope. Brilliant!

The exercise involved me taking out a rope and laying it out in front of the classroom. Then I would take two members of the audience who worked in the same department and put them at one end of the rope. Next I would take two other members of the audience who also worked together but in a different department than the first two people, and I would place them at the other end of the rope. I would then tell the first pair that for them to win they would have to get the other pair at the opposite end of the rope on their side of the room. Next, I would turn to the other team and explain that for them to win they must do the same: get the first pair at the opposite end of the rope on their side of the room. Essentially, I had set up a corporate game of tug of war.

Then I would say, "GO!"

Oh, the humanity of it all.

I would watch as four intelligent corporate leaders, some dressed in Hugo Boss and Donna Karan, pulled with all their might against each other.

Note to self: generally only sales executives were dressed in designer labels. Operations executives were often dressed in less flashy apparel. Just another example of "the man" keeping us operations people down.

Images of personal injury lawsuits would flash through my head as I witnessed the force with which the participants pulled. The four executives, straining under the effort to achieve victory, would ultimately wind up with the worst of all results. The dreaded tie. No winners.

At every organization it was the same result: tremendous effort, no advantage. I would go into more detail but I still fear reprisal from the CIA.

That was my week...until Friday. Friday changed everything.

It was the Friday gig that was the most incredible. Friday involved the Lollipop Guild.

Well, not the original guild, not the ones from *The Wizard of Oz*, but a group that was virtually identical. This guild was the Orlando Astros: fourteen kids--four, five, and six-years-old--assembled to play tee-ball. I was their coach, their mentor, their guide through the journey of baseball. Friday was our first ever practice--our first steps along this wondrous path. Clearly, I was psyched.

I volunteered to coach tee-ball because I wanted to get more involved in my community. Since I generally get upset when exposed to people who are suffering physical pain, emotional duress, or economic crisis; and since I am not particularly good at fundraising, administration, or project management, my options for community service are significantly limited. My two options at that time were picking up roadside trash or coaching baseball. Picking up trash did have a certain attraction, but I know baseball, I told myself, and I am an educator of sorts, so youth baseball seemed to be my niche.

My first official act as "Coach Mitchell" was to construct my objectives for the season. As I walked onto that baseball field at 5:00 P.M. that Friday in March 1999, the Central Florida sun slowly making its way toward the horizon, I mentally reviewed my vision for the season. Ah, yes, the Orlando Astros, these exuberant, earnest and dedicated future leaders would learn, from me, the beauty of our national past-time. We would explore the strategies and tactics that make baseball the most cerebral and intricate of all sports. We would examine the subtleties and nuances hidden beneath the surface of the game. Most importantly, we would discover the life lessons that play out between those two chalk lines: the metaphors and analogies for success that translate into the intangible that will serve these youngsters for a lifetime, all shared by a sage educator of savvy adults.

I would be molding minds.

That was my vision at 5:00 P.M....

...by 5:20 P.M. I had changed my goals. My new purpose was more singular and pure. My new vision was to return 14 children to their parents promptly at 6:00 P.M. I didn't even care if the parent received the same child they had dropped off. To me, my responsibility was the accuracy of the numbers.

"Here you go, Mrs. Khoury. Bobby had a great practice."

"Hey, this isn't Bobby!" responds a disconcerted Mrs. Khoury.

"Just take him. This kid is better looking than Bobby anyway. You traded up."

By 5:40 P.M. a horrifying realization had descended upon me like a famished vulture plucking the carcass of a dead opossum. (I tend to become a drama queen in times of personal duress.) I had run out of things to do. I had run out of things to do a full 20 minutes before practice was over! I had to fill 20 more minutes of time with these "baseball players" before I could hand them back to their parents. TWENTY MINUTES! Could we run the bases for 20 minutes? Unlikely. Could I bear to watch them attempt to catch, throw, or hit for another 20 minutes? Certainly not. Could I end practice 20 minutes early? Are you kidding me? Those parents won't be back for their kids one second before 6:00 P.M.! I racked my brain for something, anything to entertain these kids. Then it hit me.

In the back of my car was the rope.

Lots of applications for that rope went through my mind.

Many involved Bobby Khoury.

But I made the right choice. I spread the rope out behind the pitcher's mound and in front of second base and I waved all my little sluggers into the infield. As 28 eyes watched me intently, I explained the rules of this game we were about to play. Just like I had done at AT&T, General Electric, the CIA, and countless other corporate institutions, I pitted two teams of two kids against each other on opposing sides of that rope. I explained to each team that they would need to get the other team on their side of the rope to win. Just as I had done hundreds of times before, I yelled, "GO!" and waited for the stalemate.

The stalemate never happened.

They switched sides.

It took them about seven seconds. I think six seconds were spent on them trying to convince themselves there must be more to this game than that.

As I stood there with my lower jaw grazing the infield dirt in disbelief, those four kids, with only a moments hesitation, switched sides. Now, they stood staring at me with a look of overwhelming boredom until Bobby Khoury said, "Do you have any other games, Coach? That one's kinda lame."

Right then it hit me. I wasn't going to teach these kids about baseball. Heck, no. They were going to teach me. They were going to teach me about baseball and about life. I thought I knew baseball. I didn't know baseball. I didn't know that the baseball glove is perfectly designed for the transport of dirt from third base to second base. They taught me that.

I didn't know the importance of the dandelion to the game of baseball. If a dandelion, with all its seeds intact, exists anywhere on the field, it must be personally inspected by each player and then the seeds must be ceremoniously blown into the wind. Until this takes place, no other action can occur on the playing field.

I didn't know how important it was to celebrate. Oh sure, if you come back from a huge deficit, win the pennant with a "walk-off" home-run, beat the favored team in extra innings, knock yourself out celebrating. But these kids taught me a whole new criterion for celebrations. In the unlikely event that an opposing player should happen to hit a ball in fair territory, that is such cause for raucous and joyous celebration that each and every player on our team must chase after that ball and attempt to touch it; even if it means tackling your own teammate to do this. This, of course, causes a 15-minute delay in action while I meticulously replace all the players in their defensive positions.

By the way, there are no conventional baseball positions in tee-ball. No first baseman, second baseman, third baseman, shortstop or the like. Nay, nay, Nelly. In tee-ball, there are flight patterns. You study the most likely paths that a batted ball will travel and you place as many players as possible in the way of this path. Then, when the ball strikes one of your players, you yell, "Nice stop, Billy. Stop crying and throw the ball to first!"

I didn't know about the language of the game, either. Oh, I thought I did. I watch Sportscenter on ESPN. I stay up on the current jargon of the game. I pride myself in my knowledge of the latest and coolest home-run calls and street slang. Yet, clearly I did not know the language of this game. That became clear during our first game of the season.

Now, you need to know that I am an aggressive coach, particularly when it comes to base-running strategy. I believe that you put pressure on the opposing team's defense to make the play. Until the other team shows they can perform in the field effectively, you keep taking the extra base. Well, we played the Orioles in our first game and I had cast a keen eye upon their defensive execution. I found their play lacking. It was then I decided to become aggressive on the base paths.

I coached third. I coached third because I like to be involved in the game--a critical on-field decision maker influencing the action in the moment. I also coached third because I could only get one other parent to help me with the team and he coached first, but that is beside the point. Anyway, we were batting and Bobby Khoury was on second base. Bobby was a fleet-footed five-year-old with good instincts. I knew, based on my painstaking observations and scouting of the Orioles defense, that he could score on a ball hit just about anywhere in the field. I yelled out to Bobby to be alert. He immediately stopped playing in the dirt around second base and looked around for some reason to actually be alert.

Then it happened. The ball was hit slowly to the right side of the infield. I knew immediately that Bobby could score on this slow-roller. As if shot out of a cannon, Bobby came toward me. Without hesitation, calling upon my many years of baseball experience, I screamed, "GO HOME!"

He left.

It turns out that Bobby Khoury lived three blocks from the ballpark. He sprinted the entire way to his house. While I was disappointed in our miscommunication, I took a special delight in seeing him hustle. That, to me, was evidence of good coaching.

I spent 45 minutes on the phone with his mother explaining that he had not been kicked off the team. I wondered if Joe Torre ever faced these types of dilemmas with players.

These kids also taught me about life. They loved to play. They rooted for each other. They even rooted for the other team. They weren't competing so much as they were having fun and doing the best they could. That's why they didn't pull against each other in the rope exercise. It never dawned on them that they were competing. I had explained what they needed to achieve to win and they immediately recognized that each team's objectives could be accomplished simultaneously. In the words of Stephen Covey, they created a win-win situation. Now, I don't know what kids today are reading in kindergarten, but I find it hard to believe that Covey's *Seven Habits of Highly Effective People* would be on their list.

That was my epiphany.

Somehow between the ages of six-years-old and adulthood we forget something. I have been hired numerous times to build teamwork. I think these events have merit and my family certainly appreciates the income derived by my efforts to help companies enhance teamwork. But lately I have been re-evaluating the value of teamwork. With the rugged economic environment that accompanied the new millennium, most of the ineffectual teams were fired or restructured. Effective teamwork became widespread due to this Darwinian effect. The problem isn't teamwork.

The problem is **seamwork**. Seamwork is something that my Orlando Astros understood inherently and that most adults simply do not. Seamwork is different from teamwork. Seamwork is the ability to cooperate despite the boundaries that separate you. Seamwork stretches beyond departmental lines, divisional organizational charts, and borders on a map. Seamwork succeeds in the midst of differences.

To illustrate this, think of a patchwork quilt. Each little piece of fabric within the quilt is strong. Each piece is beautiful, unique, and SMALL. It cannot accomplish much of great importance because of its diminutive size. However, when these pieces of fabric are sewn together they make a quilt.

A quilt can accomplish so much more. The effectiveness, the strength of this quilt, will be largely the result of the quality of the seams.

It is the same in the corporate world. The vast majority of companies that I have worked with have excellent teamwork within the individual departments of the organization. The problems are far more likely to be in the seams, those areas where the different departments are linked. It is in the seams of an organization that the company feels the impact of the rope exercise-- for instance, sales pulling against operations and vice versa. Corporations compete against themselves far more often than they compete against their competition.

The same can be said with our communities, perhaps even our world. We operate under the assumption that to allow another to win automatically makes us lose. But helping others win doesn't make you a loser. Quite the opposite. Think about how you feel when someone wins at your expense. You immediately want the chance to "get even". Winning at someone else's expense would lead to being surrounded by losers who are consumed by the desire to get even with you. This kind of winning is not sustainable.

Conversely, creating winners all around you insures you will be surrounded by people who want nothing more than to help you succeed. That's what those kids taught me: focusing on what you can do to contribute to the success of others is the best way to insure success for yourself. That is the concept of **seamwork** in a nutshell.

Now, I remind you that I spent a great deal of time in the corporate world and I saw my share of rising stars who stepped on the heads of their colleagues to reach greater success. But looking back, I don't remember any who could maintain that success. In the words of one of my favorite philosophers, Lowell George, the lead singer of *Little Feat*: "The same dudes you abuse on the way up, you will meet up with on the way down." (From the song "On the Way Down," by Allen Toussaint, off the album *Dixie Chicken*, Warner Brothers Records, 1973, side 1/track 4.) Music is one of my filters, remember?

My brother-in-law, Russ, who should have been born during the time of the great philosophers like Plato or Socrates, once said, "Dave, I think when a man dies, if the people that he knew in life remember him with kind thoughts, then that person is in heaven. And if they remember him as a son-of-a-bitch, well then, he is in hell." The fact that Russ was liquored up at the time does not diminish the genius of that simple insight.

Maybe the key to heaven's gate is promoting **seamwork**. Certainly, a large component of personal happiness is postively sewing yourself into the fabric of the lives of others.

CHAPTER SIX

Carl Jung and the Muppets

UNDERSTANDING HUMAN BEHAVIOR

After college I worked briefly for the CBS television network. While that may sound impressive to some, it is worth noting that the station I worked at was in Terre Haute, Indiana. Now, before I have an entire city of Larry Bird loyalists screaming obscenities at me, please understand that I respect Terre Haute. The rather pungent odors of the Wabash River aside, Terre Haute was a major improvement in culture for a young man raised in Greenup, Illinois. I have nothing but the highest regard for the city and have often ordered my compact discs from this record club capital of the world. How can someone who loves music not hold a special place in his heart for a city that serves as the headquarters for a company that will send him 11 CDs for just a penny? Still, having since been exposed to many other cities in the world, Terre Haute has moved rather significantly down my personal list of favorite destinations. But, I digress.

As it turned out, broadcast journalism wasn't my cup of tea and I left this job to embark on a journey of self-discovery. Two months into my journey, I discovered myself behind the photo-development counter at a local Osco Drug store wearing a ratty company issued smock and placing price tags on cosmetic products. It wasn't quite what I had envisioned. Chicks didn't dig it either.

A couple of other dead-end jobs followed. The most memorable of this otherwise completely forgettable period of my career was my job as a videographer for a "talent agency" that traveled from town to town. Their advertisements said they could help get people on *Star Search* by providing them with an audition tape that highlighted their "talent." I use the quotation marks because much of the "talent" that was uncovered by the "talent agency" involved adult dance routines (read "strippers"). While that might sound like a pretty sweet gig for a 22-year-old boy/man, my rural Midwestern upbringing ensured that my modesty, naiveté, and general discomfort with this dynamic would preclude any possibility of enjoyment.

My rigid and repressed upbringing, combined with the requirement to occasionally work as a canvasser for the owner's other business, an aluminum-siding company, ended my brief stint in the "talent" discovery field. For those who may not be familiar with the term "canvasser," this is the person who goes door to door in a neighborhood and tries to tactfully convince people that their otherwise fabulous but ugly house would benefit by having aluminum-siding installed. While I certainly could see the value, I had no aptitude for this type of work. On top of that, I was troubled by the premise that owning an aluminum-siding company qualified a person to run a talent agency.

I also had no aptitude or interest in my dad's heating and air conditioning business. Of course every time my next new job became my next ex-job, I would land back under a house or in an attic installing ductwork for Dad's business. Each time I returned, I would think perhaps I could be happy running the family business. About three days later I would remember why I couldn't be happy doing Dad's business for long. It was a nagging combination of no aptitude and no desire to install ductwork for a living.

Eventually, I found myself entertaining the idea of traveling across the country with a friend of mine, who convinced me (or I convinced him, I can't recall) that we could finance this Kerouac-like adventure by doing odd jobs in each town we would temporarily call base. I am not sure how we came up with this plan, but I do know it seemed more exciting and reasonable when we engaged in the consumption of substances that altered our judgment.

Helpful tip: it is probably a good indication of the viability (or lack thereof) of a life strategy if you find that it seems more exciting and reasonable when you are under the influence of something that is not available in a drug store, even if it can be purchased from a slightly shady stock person from the back of the drug store's loading dock.

Anyway, somehow my sister got wind of this newest development in my career planning and intervened. My sister, being 17 years older than I am and a master's level guidance counselor, felt perhaps there might be some other options worth exploring before choosing the Kerouac one. Begrudgingly, my friend and I accepted her invitation to come to Chicago and house-sit her home over the summer while we looked for work. (Just in case I never told you, Sis, you significantly and positively changed my life with that one offer. Thank you.)

It was in Chicago that I decided to accept a position with the Platt Music Corporation, an electronics retailer who sold their merchandise through retail department stores transparently. What I mean by "transparently" is that if you went into a Marshall Field's store in Chicago and bought an appliance or stereo, you were actually buying it from Platt. So, in a way, I worked for Marshall Field's. It was later that I formally accepted a training position with Marshall Field's.

Anyway, with the new job came a new apartment, a nasty little thing that possessed the cockroaches I refer to in the preface to this book. A new era had dawned. An era that I will never forget.

I've tried.

I ate Underwood's Chicken Spread and Red Baron Pizza every day except Sunday and Monday.

I went to the Beacon Tap (I called it the Bacon Tip when I had stayed too long) every night and invented Ranch Doritos by dipping the nacho cheese versions in ranch dressing. Unfortunately, I never received proper recognition for this discovery. I would stay at the Beacon Tap until the bartender started to look attractive. That would take awhile.

I went to my sister's every Sunday and had dinner and brought home leftovers that I ate on Monday.

I did my job.

My new job was as a customer service representative (CSR). I was pretty excited. Here I was in Chicago, the windy city (actually the warehouse where I worked was in Des Plaines), working at Marshall Field's (actually Platt Music Corporation) and making $4.00--count'em, one, two, three, four dollars--EVERY hour (before taxes). It was heady stuff. Of course, they don't explain to you what a CSR does when they offer you the job. If they did, no one would take it.

I still remember walking in my first day. There was a feeling of foreboding, of eyes measuring me as I made my way to the two desks that faced each other in the middle of the open area of that warehouse office. It was almost like the people in the other departments were whispering, "Dead man walking." It wasn't until later that I discovered all the people in the delivery department, the parts department, the extended service plan department-- all of which formed a circle around customer service--had all spent time in customer service. They had either escaped or been paroled.

You see Marshall Field, the man, wrote a book called *Give the Lady What She Wants*. When I was there, the Marshall Field's customer service philosophy was extremely customer friendly. Sales associates were not allowed to tell a customer, "No." If a sales associate could not please a customer, he or she would involve a department manager. Managers did everything within reason, sometimes beyond reason, to keep the discerning customer of Marshall Field's happy. If the department manager also failed to pacify the customer, then the store manager would intervene with even more latitude to please the customer. If a customer's demands or demeanor was SO outlandish, SO incredibly unreasonable, SO nasty and uncivilized that none of these individuals could please them, then that person was referred to customer service.

Me.

Me and Jim Henson.

No, not the Muppets guy. Jim Henson was a five-year veteran of Marshall Field's electronics customer service department. He had watched others come and go, but he had stayed. His loyalty to the department had been rewarded with burnout--massive, extensive burnout--the type of burnout that can only be achieved by combining talent, compassion and drive with equal amounts of frustration. Jim Henson was talented. He was also tired. Jim was deep-fried to a crackly crunch.

For five years Jim had answered his phone knowing that the person on the other side of this impending conversation was irrational, angry, and near violence. For five years Jim had worked hard to reconcile these conflicts. Now, Jim was a crispy-critter. Jim was the kind of guy--cynical, gruff and belligerent in the way that people who know too much and have experienced too much can be--that other employees avoided.

Me, fresh off the turnip truck (or more accurately, the Greenup truck) and Jim Henson. Me, with the goofy smile of the eternally-clueless, and Jim with the perpetual scowl of the eternally-disgusted. We were quite the team.

And it worked. Initially I would listen in horror as I heard Jim manhandle a customer. At this level of interaction, the company didn't really care if we kept the person as a customer so long as the senior level executives didn't have to deal with them. Hence, Jim was free to resolve these issues as he saw fit, provided that the resolution was final. His side of the conversation might sound like this:

(phone rings)

"Henson," barks Jim as he breathlessly snatches the phone and does his best drill sergeant impression.

(listening)

"Is this going to be a long story, because I am very busy?" Jim grows impatient with the detailed story of past events that the customer feels compelled to share.

"Well, I don't like your attitude either, so we're on the same page there," Jim's eyes rolling involuntarily.

"Sure, I would be happy to transfer you to my manager. I'd be ecstatic just to get you off of my line."

And with that, Jim would extend the phone across his desk towards mine and state, "Mitchell, wanna be my manager?" It was more of a command than a request.

In that way my education on the fine art of service recovery began. Jim and I worked those phones madly. Occasionally, Jim would irritate a customer to such near psychotic levels of mental anguish that they would threaten to fling themselves into the window display of our downtown State Street store, and then he would transfer the call to me. That left me, all-mellow-farm-boy, to talk them off the ledge. I was all that, with a bag of chips and a dill pickle on the side. Until Ozzie. Ozzie Hasham. My personal anti-Christ.

OZZIE, JOHN CLEESE, AND BEHAVIORAL VIRUS INFECTIONS

You know how sometimes when you meet someone for the very first time you are immediately drawn to that person. The connection you experience with this complete stranger is immediate and strong. It is an amazing feeling to establish that instant rapport with someone. Then, of course, there is the opposite. Those occasions when you meet someone for the very first time and you feel a deep sense of repulsion. A feeling comes over you that indicates that if you never interacted with this person ever again, that would be okay. Ozzie Hasham fell distinctly into this latter category for me.

It started on a Monday. Ozzie had purchased some merchandise at our big warehouse sale over the weekend. The warehouse sale was our annual de-evolution into the retail equivalent of crack-cocaine dealing. Items were priced insanely cheap to unload them and shoppers descended on this event with the frothing mouth and darting eyes of a hardened addict three days past his last fix. Despite our best efforts to label every item "AS IS", the week following a warehouse sale was always mayhem in customer service. Customers calling wanting owner's manuals, turntable cartridges, connecting cables...and each armed with the assurances of a haggard sales associate who had told them these items were available by calling customer service. These were the same sales associates who had been procured from a temp agency two days before the event and told explicitly, "Whatever you do, don't promise a freaking turntable cartridge to these people." That was the entirety of their training.

Ozzie initially called about a remote control for his stereo system.

My recollection of the events that followed that first call are decidedly hazy. Much like the post-traumatic-stress-syndrome suffered by soldiers, I cannot remember distinctly what happened next. I do recall that the frequency of Ozzie's calls to me increased as the week progressed. It seems to me that the nature of his demands kept shifting as well. In my memory, Ozzie's original request broadened and shifted until, by Thursday, I could no longer tolerate any more interactions with Mr. Hasham. To me, the process of satisfying Ozzie Hasham bore an uncomfortable similarity to a snipe hunting trip I had experienced when I was eleven-years-old. Our final conversation was brief.

"Mr. Hasham," my voice raising and becoming higher in pitch, the latter quality an annoying by-product to my anger, "I don't think you know what you want. And until you figure out what is going to make you happy, I don't want you to call me ever again!" With that I slammed down the phone, hanging up in anger for the first time in my life.

Jim Henson leapt out of his chair in excitement. "THAT"S the way you talk to them! You're learning, boy. You've got potential. Now, you just need to do that on MONDAY, cause you're wasting time."

I remember feeling equal parts mad and embarrassed. "He deserved it," I said to myself, more to convince myself than anyone else. "Asshole."

After a few minutes I regained my composure and answered my phone again. "Marshall Field's Electronics Department, Customer Service. This is Dave. How may I help you?"

"May I speak to the manager please?"

Like I wouldn't recognize Ozzie Hasham's voice after a week's worth of phone conversations. "Of course. It would be my pleasure."

And then I looked across my desk at Jim Henson. "Jim, would you like to be MY manager?" I would show Ozzie, I thought to myself. He had the good cop. Now he's gonna get Jim Henson. He'll be begging for me. He didn't know how good he had it.

Jim's eyes widened as I made my offer. He had the look of a hungry lion moments before the raw meat is thrown into his cage. I even noticed a tiny bit of saliva trickling down the corner of his mouth. "Really?" Jim responded with a barely contained level of excitement that bordered on manic. "Put him through!"

I transferred the call to Jim and then sank back in my chair to await the pyrotechnics. My God, I thought to myself, this has the makings of a World Wrestling Federation Smackdown Main Event. Let's get ready to rrrrruuuuu ummmmmmbbbbbbllllle!

What happened next rivaled the UFO sighting I experienced in high school with my very good friend, Scott Shafer.

The Jim Henson I had worked with for the past year, the cantankerous burn-out who dispatched unhappy customers with the ease of a pest control professional, THAT Jim Henson disappeared. He was replaced by what George Bush #1 would have described as a kinder, gentler Jim.

"Good afternoon, Customer Service. This is Jim. How may I help you?" There was practically a lilt in his voice for Chrissake!

"Well, I am so sorry to hear that, Mr. Hasham. No, no, that is certainly not our policy. I don't know why this has been so difficult for you. Of course I wil. I will have that done for you today. Yes, I know Dave Mitchell. Well, Mr Hasham, not everyone is cut out for customer service."

As I listened to Jim's half of the conversation astonished and incredulous, it began to occur to me what was happening. Within 15 minutes, Jim had resolved a customer conflict that I had been working on for a week. Jim got a letter from Mr. Hasham, a letter that detailed for two paragraphs how fantastic Jim Henson was to work with. A letter he never showed to our boss, Shirley Guagenti, because it went into great detail in paragraph three about how horrible Dave Mitchell was. But Jim kept that letter in his top drawer and anytime I would start to get a bit full of myself, Jim would pull that letter out and say, "Remember Mr. Hasham, Dave? He didn't like you much, did he?"

As I watched Jim so effectively handle Ozzie Hasham, I realized that I must have contributed (perhaps created completely) this conflict. Now, there was no denying that Ozzie and I were two very different people. In Jungian psychological terms, it could be said that our interactive styles were exactly opposite. But that doesn't excuse my poor handling of the situation.

By the way, the concept of interactive styles is of keen interest to me. I am not going to delve into this complicated issue in this book, but I do enjoy speaking on this issue. In fact, I present Jungian psychological concepts on human interaction using different themes like Hollywood movie icons or wine-tasting events. These sessions are among my most popular seminars. I mention this because I love doing these seminars, make a large percentage of my income doing these seminars, and hope that you, as the reader of this book, may be in a position to hire me to do one of these seminars in the future. If this whole paragraph strikes you as gratuitous marketing and self-promotion, then you have interpreted its intent correctly. My children may well be sucking on washcloths for nourishment as you read this. Please hire me. Now, back to Live and Learn, or Die Stupid...

Besides the obvious difference between my style and Ozzie's, there were other reasons why my interaction with Mr. Hasham went awry. About a year later came the epiphany. This three-part epiphany was so simple, that I am almost ashamed to share it with you. It could damage my credibility--provided, of course, that I have any credibility with you.

Moving forward about a year, I was now working as a store-trainer for Marshall Field's. It's funny now to look back on this period of my career. That job was my first real training position. I would provide training to the sales associates on how to run the cash register primarily, with some customer service skills thrown in--the same classes, the same content, day in and day out. I became so familiar with the content that I would often have out-of-body experiences while conducting classes. There I would be, hovering over the classroom, contemplating my weekend plans or grocery list, while simultaneously explaining how to process a credit-card purchase being sent out-of-state as a gift. In fact, during one class, not only did I drift away during my presentation, but I also tapped my purple flipchart marker incessantly against my hand. The result of this feverish tapping was a splatter pattern of fluorescent purple on the front of my crisp white shirt. At the lunch break, a thoughtful student pointed out the distracting behavior. I remember that day as being particularly influential in the development of my professional self-esteem. I shudder to think of the quality of those sessions.

Anyway, during the two-day cash register training class, there was a segment on customer service. The bulk of this segment was dedicated to a videotape. I no longer remember the title of the videotape, but I do know that the British comedic actor John Cleese starred in it and his company produced it. The tape was clever as you would expect from a Cleese influenced project, even one produced for the purpose of customer service education. The learning points were interwoven around a faux murder mystery. My three epiphanies mirrored the three major points about human behavior:

1. Behavior breeds behavior.
2. You choose your behavior.
3. Positive behavior overcomes negative behavior.

These concepts probably strike you as incredibly obvious. Nonetheless, I am going to explain them. It is what we speakers do, explain the obvious at length.

Behavior breeds behavior. I remember hearing about a study once, probably by Johns Hopkins since they seem to do almost all the noteworthy studies, on the source of stress for people while at work. The study concluded that the most prominent source of stress at work was interaction with other people. Duh. Big bag of duh! My dad, the appliance repairman, used to tell me this all the time when I was a youngster. He put it this way: "The world would be a wonderful place if it weren't for people."

Anyway, what "behavior breeds behavior" means is simply this: The way we treat someone has a huge bearing on the way that person will treat others. Put another way, if I am in a bad mood and treat someone else poorly, there is a good chance that this person will, in turn, now be in a bad mood and treat the next person accordingly. In this regard, my bad mood is like a viral infection. With each personal contact I have with another person, I spread my infected mood. I am the Typhoid Mary of behavior.

Conversely, the opposite is true. If I am in a good mood, my interactions with others impact them in a good way. In this scenario I am spreading joy. I like spreading joy and that gets us to the second point.

By the way, I notice that some people mistrust joy-spreaders. Have you noticed this? Often, when I am walking around with a smile on my face, making eye contact with others, and complimenting them, the response I get involves a furrowed eye brow, a quickening of someone's pace and short, and anxiety-filled replies. Maybe it's my technique.

You choose your behavior. Certainly the way you are treated by others can influence what behavior you choose, but ultimately the choice is still yours. I mean, have you ever been in a good mood? (If you answer this question with a "no," slowly put down this book, walk deliberately to the phone, calmly dial your local crisis center, and start your life anew.) Sure you have. How about the opposite? Have you ever been in a bad mood? Boy, howdy! So you know that your mood is not something you are born with. It is something you choose (unless you are suffering from depression or another mental health concern, and that is a far more complicated issue).

Barring health issues, our behavior is under our control. We make choices about our behavior based on internal and external influences, but the final decision is ours. Now, which state would you rather be in, a good mood or a bad mood? I'm thinking you'd rather be in a good mood. So why aren't we always in a good mood? Factors. External factors. Like other people. Sure, I completely understand. Having said that, reread the first chapter on *internal locus of control*. Be the hand and choose a good mood, because good moods are so much better than bad ones. That moves us to the third point.

Positive behavior overcomes negative behavior. Because healthy people would prefer to be in a good mood rather than a bad mood, positive behavior has an innate advantage over negative behavior. That means that if two people were interacting, one in a good mood and the other in a bad mood, eventually the one in a bad mood would convert to a good mood. Now, this doesn't always happen because you don't know how committed to the bad mood this other person is. However, one thing is for certain. If the good mood person gives up and lets the other person breed his behavior, therefore putting both of them in a bad mood, there is a whole new level of ugly behavior possible. Bottom line, even if your good mood doesn't convert the other person's bad mood, your good mood will at least help keep the bad mood from getting worse.

Now, back to Ozzie Hasham. Ozzie was in a bad mood. He had received what he considered to be poor service and had chosen a negative behavior as a result. That's not unusual. I initially tried to influence Ozzie's behavior with my positive behavior. Unfortunately the "behavior breeds behavior" phenomenon works both ways, and since Ozzie was more committed to his negative behavior than I was to my positive behavior, ultimately his behavior won. I became negative. Once I became negative, he went to a new, deeper level of negativity. I followed, and on it went into the abyss of conflict.

Enter Jim Henson. Because Jim wanted to cover my back, he was extremely committed to his positive behavior. Soon, Ozzie (who, like all healthy people, wanted desperately to be in a good mood) became influenced by Jim's good mood. The spiral that had gone down when Ozzie and I had interacted was now moving upward. Within a few minutes, Jim had resolved the issue.

Now, like I said, the different interactive styles that we all possess certainly have a huge impact on our interpersonal relationships. There are several great books about these issues. Heck, maybe I will write one if this one sells more than the handful of copies that I plan to buy personally. But no matter how well-versed we become on matters Jungian, I still believe that one of the best road maps for handling other people is the one that John Cleese taught me when I was about 23-years-old.

Behavior breeds behavior. You can choose your behavior. Positive behavior overcomes negative behavior.

Try it.

CHAPTER SEVEN

When Your Mojo Goes

SENSE OF HUMOR

Have you ever been a senior in high school? I have a theory about this crazy, complicated time. If you want to know what degree of cockiness you are capable of achieving, go back and examine your behavior during this time. I mean, come on, you've waited years for this. Freshman year, you are just a frightened little bunny trying to melt into the walls of high school. Though sophomore year feels a little bit better, the fact that there are still more kids older rather than younger than you can be intimidating. Junior year is like being the runner-up in a beauty contest: "Should the seniors be unable to fulfill their duties as seniors, the juniors will reign." Finally, senior year arrives. Boo-yah.

I had been honorable mention all-conference first baseman my junior year. Unmistakably, the entire purpose of baseball season my senior year was *my* pursuit of first team all-conference first baseman. Clearly, because the entire world was all about *me*. The only snag was we got a new baseball coach my senior year. Bob Gaddey. Apparently Coach Gaddey did not receive the advance publicity kit I had sent him in the mail. It was also apparent that Coach Gaddey was unaware that the entire world was all about *me*.

Coach Gaddey arrived at our school with a list of priorities for the baseball season. He gathered us together and shared some lunacy about teamwork and individual sacrifices for the greater good of the team. Whatever! Not one mention of *the* most important goal, *my* pursuit of first team all-conference first baseman.

This disparate opinion of the purpose of the baseball season came to an ugly apex during the fourth game of the season. We, the Cumberland Pirates, were playing the Martinsville Blue Streaks at Haughton Park in Greenup, Illinois. Both teams were 3 - 0, each having won two non-conference games and one conference game. This was an early battle for advantage in the hotly contested Little Illini Conference. You probably remember it? Spring 1979? It was in the Greenup Press, the weekly four-page newspaper. Sound familiar? Well, anyway, the story follows.

It's the bottom of the fifth inning. We're trailing 3 – 2. There is one out and a runner on first. I am coming to the plate. I bat third in the lineup. If you know anything about baseball, you know the third hitter has good power, good speed: probably your best natural athlete on the team.

Short pause here for the reader to realize that the preceding sentence should be perceived with the self-mocking sarcasm the writer intends.

As I step into the batter's box, I immediately begin my pre-at-bat ritual, all carefully designed to impress my girlfriend.

I dig in with my left foot (I am left-handed.) while keeping my right foot out of the batter's box, all the time surveying the positioning of all the fielders. It's a move that suggests I have such bat control that I can place a batted ball anywhere I want. I then bend down and pick up a handful of dirt, rubbing it onto my bat, onto my hands, and finally onto my pants. The first two are to improve my grip, the latter placement of dirt, onto my pants, is so if I fail to get on base during the game it will still appear as if I am an integral part of the action. (I was a very cerebral ballplayer.) Finally, I look down at Coach Gaddey at third base to give the appearance of getting a sign--a move I do as a formality because Coach Gaddey likes to feel involved in the game. It is my way of feigning respect.

With a runner on first and my power to the gaps, I can foresee scalding the first-belt high fastball into the right-center field grass and driving home the tying run. Heck, I might even jack that cheese-heater the Martinsville pitcher calls a "fastball" right over the right-field fence. Would you like honey, Mr. Pooh? Bring me a platter of your finest meats and cheeses! I can already imagine my picture on the front page of the Greenup Press.

My fantasy is harshly interrupted by the realization that Coach Gaddey has just rubbed his forearms (what we called "the sleeves"). This is the indicator sign. In baseball, there are signs that indicate there will be a sign. It is a very complicated sport.

Coach Gaddey follows "the sleeves" by touching his nose. Four letters in nose. Four letters in bunt. We aren't a bright bunch, so Coach Gaddey keeps the signs simple. He has given *me*, former honorable mention all-conference first baseman, senior, three-hole hitter, the BUNT sign. HELLO! I don't bunt. Freshmen bunt. Nine-hole hitters bunt. Not me. I don't even practice bunting. Shoot, I would have to look up bunt in the dictionary to spell it. I think bunt is a cake.

Well, dutifully, I square to bunt the first pitch. The pitcher fires a juicy, belt-high, fastball over the plate and I bunt it foul down the first base line. Now down 0 - 1 in the count, I know I am going to get some off-speed junk, probably a hook (that's baseball talk for a curveball) on the outside corner. "I ain't gonna hit his pitch," I say to myself, steeling my determination to lay off the junk and work the count back into my favor. As I complete my at-bat ritual, my eyes again meet Coach Gaddey's. Coach has now moved about a third of the way down the baseline and, more emphatically, signals for the bunt.

I respond with the "possessed pigeon" look. You know, that look pigeons get when they bob their head and bob their heads and then all of the sudden, out of the blue, cock their head back, set their gaze on something, and freeze. Weird. I always assumed it was some sort of demonic possession. Anyway, I am in utter disbelief. I shoot a glance to my comrades on the bench to see if they are witnessing this unfurling melodrama, but they are all experimenting with chewing tobacco and are too light headed to realize what is happening.

Again, I dutifully square to bunt. A lazy Uncle Charlie (That's more baseball talk for curve-ball--ain't baseball cool?) floats across the outside edge of the plate and I bunt it foul down the third base line. Now down 0-2 in the count I realize that I will have to give up my desire to drive a pitch into the gap. I can expect a steady diet of pitches that are high, low, outside or inside in an effort to entice me to swing at a bad pitch. My thought now is to battle off these pitches and try to work the count to full. I will try to take a pitch the other way, a single over the shortstop perhaps, and advance the runner, allowing my clean-up hitting teammate to experience the glory of driving in the tying and winning run. All of this is running through my mind. I don't even look for a sign from Coach Gaddey. I don't have to. He has now moved two thirds of the way down the third base line and is screaming at the top of his lungs, "BUNT THE GODDAMN BALL, MITCHELL!", in front of the entire student body of Cumberland High School.

Actually, there were only about 12 people there, most of them parents, but I like to remember the story as involving the entire student body.

In that moment, I make a decision--a decision that will change my life.

I don't bunt.

I don't even try to hit the ball.

I decide to draw the line right then. As the next pitch approaches the plate (low and inside) I flail at it, obviously intending on missing it. I then glare down the third base line at Coach Gaddey, drop the bat, whirl around on my heel like Baryshnikov, and return to the bench.

I remained on the bench for the next five games serving a suspension for insubordination.

Immediately after I decided on this strategy, I knew I had made a mistake. Still, being a typical 17-year-old boy, I was defiant. Later, when I returned home after the game, I subjected my father to what was probably a 30-minute harangue, a tirade about the injustice, the unfairness, the inequity, the evil incarnate that was Bob Gaddey.

To my dad's credit, he listened intently to my epistle. He didn't interrupt as I spewed bile for that half hour. When I was finished, Dad said, "Son, do you think you can change Bob Gaddey?"

I responded with that incredulous tone that only a teenager can truly manifest. "Noooo, I don't think I can change Bob Gaddey," came my sarcastic reply.

"Son, let me give you some advice that is gonna save you a bunch of heartache in your life."

Internally, my eyes were rolling and I sighed heavily. I say internally because I was quite afraid of my father and would not have risked inciting more anger in him by ACTUALLY rolling my eyes and sighing heavily. But I definitely did it internally.

"In life, if you can change it, change it...", he began. Funny, this sentiment is fundamentally the same thing as telling someone about the importance of an *internal locus of control*. My dad was actually an amateur behavioral psychologist disguised as an appliance repairman.

"In life, if you can change it, change it: if you can't, laugh about it. You'll be a lot happier." Then my dad launched into his own epistle. It wasn't pretty. He told me that I was selfish. That my only concern was for my needs and not the needs of others.

On top of that, he added, I had made my life so important to me that it was funny to behold as an outsider. "Oh, you are funny, Son, but not in the way you want to be." He added, "If you don't learn to laugh at yourself soon, you are going to live a very miserable life."

Have you ever caught a bad-hop grounder right in the gazeechies? If you are a woman, you don't actually have gazeechies, but you get the picture. It hurts. Gazeechies, by the way, is a word my son Slade and I made up for testicles. Testicles is an ugly word to a kid. Gazeechies, on the other hand, is funny as hell. "Funny as hell" is an important balance for the pain of being hit in the gazeechies.

I thought about what my dad told me. Just like that, within a moment . . . like, you know, within ten years or so, I got it. (Just because your parents give you good advice doesn't mean you choose to apply it immediately. I remind myself of this every time I offer my thoughts to my teen-daughter, Brooke. I am sure she is storing my wisdom away, even though it appears that she dismisses my input as if it were the ramblings of a disturbed mind.)

You have to have a sense of humor to achieve contentment. I'm not talking about telling jokes either. I'm talking about recognizing the inanity of life. In particular, our own unique contribution to life's comedy. You have to be able to laugh at yourself. My dad had hit the nail on the head. My head.

On a side note, I don't know about your dad, but my father got much smarter as I got older. By the time I was 30, the man was a freaking genius. I don't know if he was taking ginkgo or some other brain-enhancing supplement, but he really sharpened right up. It's just a shame he wasn't brighter during my adolescent years. Dad passed away about a year before this book was sent to publishing. I sure miss him. The last chapter is dedicated to the wisdom he tried to impart in me in his own unique way.

WHERE DID THE MOJO GO

Many years later, after doing a keynote speech about these concepts, a gentleman approached me as the crowd dispersed. "I really enjoyed your presentation, but I have to disagree about the importance of a sense of humor. I am a serious man." The gentleman continued, "People appreciate my no-nonsense style. I don't kid around, and for that reason, I am highly respected."

I thought about what this man said for a little while and said, "I think you are wrong." Here's why.

Some days we--you, me, everyone--roll out of bed and we got the mojo working that day. We take a shower and do our hair and it looks perfect.

There's no traffic on the way to work. A parking place is just waiting for us. We resolve each issue effectively. We offer a wonderful idea at the staff meeting. We receive a commendation from a customer. Our boss pats us on the back. An attractive person smiles at us at lunch.

We are all that, a bag of chips, and a dill pickle on the side. We rock, we're hot, we're smokin', we got a shizzle in our nizzle (by the time this book is released, that will so not be current) cause, like I said, we got the mojo working. We go home after a day like that feeling like we've got it all figured out. Then we go to bed and get up the next morning...

And we got no mo' mojo. Where did the mojo go? We have been de-mojoed overnight.

We take a shower and spend 45 minutes doing our hair only to look like we have a hornet's nest on top of our head. We are 15 minutes late for work because of traffic. There isn't a parking space for miles. Every issue that was resolved yesterday has come undone. We sit in the staff meeting in what can only be described as a catatonic stupor. Ozzie Hasham is on hold on line one for us. There is a post-it note on our office door from our boss that says simply, "SEE ME." An attractive person backs into you knocking coffee down the front of your shirt and still doesn't acknowledge you.

Like I said, we got NO mojo. In the words of Mark Knopfler (*Dire Straits* leader), "Sometimes you are the windshield, and sometimes you are the bug." Well, today, my friend, you are the bug. For the last eleven years I have made my living doing speaking engagements. I get nervous every time. Why? Because I never know when the mojo is gonna leave me. Let me tell you, if you think losing your mojo is unpleasant, try doing it with 1,000 people watching you. Talk about a gut punch.

On the bug days, you need a sense of humor. Everyone has days like this. It's not always a day. Sometimes mojo just leaves for an hour. Could be during that very important meeting. You walk in, sit down, and soon you realize, "Damn, I didn't bring my mojo." Sometimes mojo leaves for a week, usually right before you go on vacation. Messes with you. You spend the whole vacation wondering if your mojo will ever come back.

I once had a mojo-free month. Horrible.

But now I have a theory about mojo. At this point we have to capitalize the word. I believe that Mojo sometimes feels like it is taken way too much for granted. You know, Mojo just isn't getting its props. So, to get your attention, Mojo leaves. I imagine Mojo saying to itself, "Yeah, let's see how well Dave does without me. He'll be begging for his Mojo in no time. No Mojo, no standing O!"

The more desperate you become, the more you then try to hide your lack of Mojo from others, and the longer Mojo stays away. It is a vicious, ugly cycle.

On the other hand, if you can laugh at yourself, that frightens Mojo. Mojo becomes worried that you might not miss it or that you think you can do without it. Then Mojo comes rushing back to you. Consequently, the best way to shorten Mojo-free periods is to laugh at your own mojolessness.

Well, that's my theory anyway.

All I know is that a lot of the negative behaviors that I have manifested: the fear, the mistrust, the untruths--were all related to trying to conceal insecurities and weaknesses. By admitting them, heck, by laughing about them, they suddenly shrink in importance. When the insecurities shrink, so does the fear, mistrust, and untruths. The space left behind by the shrinking of our insecurities is filled by the expansion of our contentment and happiness.

So laugh. But not at others. At yourself. Besides, you have so much more material to work with that way.

CHAPTER EIGHT

Wild Monkeys in Duncan, Oklahoma

THE POWER OF THE SMILE

So many times I have waited out flight delays, ate at Burger King, arrived at hotels at 2:00 A.M. (a few times at 6:00 A.M.!), walked around airport concourses for two, three, four hours or more, and I have found myself uttering, "The glamorous life of the speaker." Occasionally when working an event with my dear friend Jerry or my good buddy Barry, this glamorous life can be more bearable. But most of the time I am alone. Alone. It is the most alone that I ever feel. I hike for hours on end in the mountains, just me and the dogs (Martini and Rossi) and I never feel alone. In my mind there is no more lonely place than an airport full of people when a person is one thousand miles from home.

"The glamorous life of the speaker."

Of course there are the cities. Cities are cool--cool when you have someone to share them with. I love to go out on date night with my wife. I love to explore the hot spots with Jerry. San Francisco, fabulous city–great food and wine. Chicago–wonderful people. Houston–so many restaurants. New Orleans–so many memories, I just wish I could remember them all. Philadelphia--even more fabulous than I expected. Baltimore–also better than I expected. Austin–oh, that music scene. Miami–man, those folks are good-looking. Atlanta–a spectacular city. St. Louis–who knew? Los Angeles–so hip. Dallas–big hair. Portland (both Maine and Oregon)–as different as their geography. I started to list all the cities I've been to, but it is far too long of a list. For every city I've been to all over North American and Europe, there are memories. Most of the memories are good, but some are lousy. I've had to make it through some long, lonely, restless nights in many of these cities.

Then there's Duncan, Oklahoma.

I don't even remember why I was in Duncan. I was speaking somewhere—Halliburton, Brown and Root, I think. I remember landing at an airport and I'm pretty sure I was in Oklahoma City. I got into a van, a sort of modern day stagecoach really, and proceeded to bounce around with a full bladder for 90 minutes till we finally arrived at the kind of spot my wife's step-mom, Bonnie, would describe as "out where God lost his shoes." (I love these kinds of phrases. I remember my dad used to describe a particularly remote area as, "...out where the hoot owls date the chickens and the roosters don't care." Still makes me giggle.)

I remember a rather unassuming Holiday Inn in Duncan, Oklahoma, and a front desk clerk who called me by name when I walked in the door because I was the last person due to check in that night. I recall a television that had poor reception leaving me with only four clear channels of viewing.

I also remember the monkeys.

The wild monkeys of Duncan, Oklahoma.

I was watching the Discovery Channel. It was one of the four channels. C-Span, CNN, and PBS were the other three, I think. Anyway, the Discovery Channel had a special on primates. As I enjoyed my Pizza Hut pizza (or maybe it was Dominos, I'm not sure), I watched with riveted attention as the narrator discussed the non-verbal communication techniques of monkeys. Monkeys, apparently, are quite the non-verbal communicators.

As I'm watching this show, they illustrate how a monkey who passes through the territory of another monkey will show with a simple facial expression that he respects the resident monkey and intends no ill-will.

The monkey smiles--an exaggerated smile.

The narrator goes on to share with viewers that this exaggerated smile is also meant to show a measure of fear, in addition to respect, to the resident monkey. This, I learn, signals to the resident monkey that the trespasser plans no attack and is merely passing through.

All of this is communicated by the monkey's Joker-like smile.

Then the view shifts to a group of people riding a roller coaster. We watch as they ascend to the top of the ride. We then see the faces of each person as they crest that peak and begin the plummet downward to what must feel like certain death. Next the camera zooms in on how each one of them is displaying that same facial expression, like an involuntary display of respect and fear for the descent.

As I continued to watch I realized that I, too, had used this non-verbal communication technique. Back when my wife and I made our decision about the size of our family, we agreed on having two children, hopefully one boy and one girl. If necessary, we would reluctantly go up to three children to have representation of both genders, but that would be the max. As soon as we achieved one boy and one girl or three children, whichever came first, I would then see a doctor to experience a certain procedure to render me incapable of fathering any more kids.

Yes, the vasectomy.

As I write this, my son, whose arrival officially fulfilled our childbearing contract, just celebrated his twelfth birthday. I have yet to get a vasectomy. When my wife reminds me of our agreement, I flash the monkey's exaggerated smile--a show of respect and fear for my wife. I'm thinking that if John Bobbitt had seen the Discovery Channel that night and used this non-verbal communication technique, things might have gone a little better with Lorena.

The narrator continued his discussion of non-verbal communication by pointing out the effect of the human smile on interpersonal dynamics. His focus now was not on the exaggerated smile to show respect and fear, but rather the natural smile. He pointed out how this less exaggerated version is used daily to show alliance and friendship to others. It is a shortcut for accessibility. It is the silent way we spread joy.

That is when the pizza nearly fell off my lap.

So blinding was the epiphany that I nearly collapsed onto the floor.

I NEED TO SMILE MORE!

MATCHING THE OUTSIDE TO THE INSIDE

During my time in the corporate world, I often received feedback from others that I was somewhat intimidating. I never understood how I could have created such a reputation. I was from Greenup, Illinois! How in the world could I be intimidating?

After the monkey documentary, I understood why. I immediately ran into the bathroom at the Holiday Inn in Duncan, Oklahoma and started making faces at myself. I tried to recreate my most common facial expressions. I scared myself.

In that moment I realized I suffered from FBS...furrowed brow syndrome. I looked intense, even intimidating. Did you see *Toy Story II*? There is a scene in that movie where Mr. Potato Head puts on his "angry eyes." That was me. For the love of Benji, I thought. No wonder people think I am intimidating. Heck, I intimidate myself!

From that day on I made a commitment to smile more. It may well be the most important commitment to personal development I have ever made. No really, I mean it--just try smiling.

Human beings are susceptible to first impressions. We can't help it. We do judge books by covers. It's true we do rush to judgment. We install filters in our mind, positive or negative, based on those first pieces of information we receive about another person, place or thing. Once that filter is in place, we have a hard time changing our perception. Despite the fact that I was a happy, easy-going guy on the inside, I looked like an intense, serious, and intimidating person on the outside. My most common facial expressions were influencing how people responded to me.

Then, just like the monkey, I would react to people's reactions to me by being even more intense, serious, and intimidating.

My common facial expressions were changing the way I felt and acted. Oddly, I had always thought it worked the other way around. But the truth is, the way we look and the way we feel and the way we act are so intertwined that when we change one of these behaviors, any one of them, it also affects the other two.

Would you rather be happy, relaxed, content, and joyous or would you prefer to be intense, restricted, stressed, and intimidating? I wanted to be the former. To do so, I decided I would spend more time looking like I felt that way.

I started smiling.

And smiling.

I practiced smiling at airports. Nobody smiles at airports. It was an amazing experience. I started to meet more pleasant people. I received better customer service. More people started conversations with me. I got upgraded more often. Bartenders bought me drinks.

I smiled at the gym. People started to remember my name. I started feeling sort of popular. People would remark that I was always in a good mood.

Nothing significant had changed in my life except that I was now making it a point to smile more often. Because of that one change of behavior, my reputation changed 180 degrees. You know what else? I felt happier. As a result of the way people were treating me, I WAS in a good mood more often--all because of a smile.

That is how powerful a smile can be.

It's hard to estimate how many people are truly happy in this world. I can confidently say, however, that there sure are a lot of people who aren't happy. I used to fantasize about being that magical genie who could grant three wishes for all of humankind. The three things I would wish for are that all people would have high self-esteem, that all people would have an ability to be resilient under stress, and that all people would smile. The first two would probably require a genie's intervention, but smiling could be accomplished immediately.

It is the simplest damn thing, but I am telling you, smiling works. I probably should have started with this suggestion, but I might have reduced my credibility even further by starting with such a fundamental notion. I figure if you have read until this point, you either have WAY too much free time, or you like what you are reading.

Either way, I encourage you to slap on a grin and notice what impact it will have on your life experience.

Just try it.

Smile.

CHAPTER NINE

Song for My Father

I am about done.

The experience of writing a book on what I have always talked about has been amazingly interesting. There's more I could say, but I'm getting tired of my own voice, so you might be, too. Plus, I need to save some stories for the sequel!

We've talked about several concepts that have helped me in my pursuit of happiness and contentment. These were:

- Internal Locus of Control
- Individual Interpreted Reality
- Positive Self Talk
- Positive Focus
- Promoting Seamwork
- Understanding Human Behavior
- Maintaining a Sense of Humor
- The Power of the Smile

These are all great concepts, at least for me. I hope something may have struck you as valuable. But to wrap up this book, I want to pay special tribute to my father.

Dad died in January 2005. He was 83-years-old. Most of his life, and the entirety of my life, he lived in Greenup, Illinois. He owned Mitchell's Heating and Air Conditioning. He coached Little League Baseball. He supported many organizations both publicly and privately. He was active in the Presbyterian Church until becoming disillusioned with the politics of it all. He fought in World War II. He married when he was 20-years-old and stayed with the same woman, despite her many troubles, until she died over 50 years later.

Most important to me, however, is this man raised me.

I found out about my father's death while speaking to a group of claims adjusters at Allstate Insurance in Roanoke, Virginia. (By the way, some of the most gracious people I have ever met were in the Roanoke office that day, including the manager, Herb Roper. I will never forget the kindness extended to me by everyone there). I left Roanoke, flew to Chicago, and drove to the funeral with my sister. The day we buried our father was brutally cold.

And no one showed up.

Oh, there were the Masons to deliver final rites and some veterans for the military salute. A couple of people who were not required to attend did show up (thank you Tim Yaw and Tim Jackson). But for a lifetime of 83 years, few people attended.

Wow, I thought, so this is what it comes down to. One's entire life can be culminated with a few words and even fewer in attendance. My grief was punctuated by the firing of the rifles and the lonely sound of "Taps" as the funeral concluded. (Man, whoever wrote "Taps" nailed it. That is one sad tune.)

The whole affair did not seem commensurate with the impact this man had on my life. Therefore, I decided to extend the tribute to my dad in my own way. Since I get to appear in front of approximately 10,000 people each year, I make it a point to include some piece of my father's wisdom in every speech I make, somehow. I also decided that whenever possible I would request "Song for My Father" by Horace Silver. (Sullivan's Steakhouse in Houston is a particularly good place to accomplish this, I found. Hey, if I'm going to honor my father, might as well throw in a well-prepared filet mignon and a nice glass of wine.)

Since I am winding down this book, let me throw out one more tribute to my father. We'll call these the "Dale-isms". Like I mentioned earlier in the book, Dad had a saying for every situation--many clichés, a few originals. Now that I am a father, I find all of these pearls of wisdom coming out of my lips directed towards my own kids. So, here's to you, Dad. I hope you are happy and content wherever you may be.

> "I love you boy, but damn..."
> "No good deed goes unpunished..."
> "Some cook, some clean and some just eat..."
> "Cheer up. It's gonna get worse..."
> "Don't try to teach a pig to dance. You'll get frustrated and the pig will get mad..."
> "I was so poor growing up that I ate nothing but jam sandwiches...You know what jam sandwiches are? Two pieces of bread jammed together."
> "Do something...even if it's wrong."
> "That guy talks like a man with a paper ass."

"He lives out where the hoot owls date the chickens and the rooster don't care."

"Act like you know what you're doing. By the time they realize you don't, you'll be gone."

"If you can change, change it. If you can't, laugh about it."

"In a hundred years, it won't matter."

"Did anyone die? Then how bad can it be."

and. . ."Son, if it makes you happy, that's all that matters."

This last one didn't pass his lips until he was quite old, and always with a soulful, prolonged, and deeply melancholy gaze. Dad, you did good, and I love you.

There have been many other extremely important people in my life. My wife Lori has been absolutely the most important person to me for over 20 years and will always hold the most special place in my heart. My children, Brooke and Slade, are amazing--sources of such pride and joy that exceed anything I could imagine. I am so lucky to have a sister that is as intelligent and caring as Diana. My dear friends, Jerry, Dennis, and Scott, are incredible people who have provided me with many shared special memories.

I have been fortunate to have worked for and with so many talented professionals: Ted Steele, Bob Atkinson, Susan Wally, Jim Henson, Max Suzenaar, Bob Stolz, Susan Meeske, to name just a few. In addition, I have had, and still have, the pleasure of working with some brilliant people as clients. The list is endless and no effort to capture all the names of those who have influenced me could be complete.

Perhaps, ultimately, that is the most important element of contentedness—the relationships that develop over time. I think it is this connectedness to each other that insulates us from the rigors of life's challenges.

As I said in the preface to this book, I am just an average guy. But I have amazing loved ones, and I am so much better as a result. So while I continue to live and learn, at the very least, I know one thing for sure: when I look around at the company I keep, I will <u>NOT</u> die stupid!

Printed in the United States
55322LVS00004BA/280-660